ESS
PSY

**General Editor
Peter Herriot**

═══ **F5** ═══

**PSYCHOLOGY
AND THE ENVIRONMENT**

ESSENTIAL

PSYCHOLOGY

PSYCHOLOGY AND THE ENVIRONMENT

Terence Lee

Methuen

First published 1976 by Methuen & Co Ltd
11 New Fetter Lane, London EC4P 4EE
© 1976 Terence Lee
Printed in Great Britain by
Richard Clay (The Chaucer Press) Ltd
Bungay, Suffolk

ISBN (hardback) 0 416 81910 9
ISBN (paperback) 0 416 81920 6

We are grateful to Grant McIntyre of
Open Books Publishing Ltd for assistance
in the preparation of this series

Contents

Editor's Introduction

Buildings are for people. Some of us look at them, others live and work in them. Hospitals, schools and houses may be beautiful to look at but hell to live in. Terence Lee shows how psychology can provide evidence as to the functions such buildings perform for those who use them. He discusses the ways in which we perceive our man-made environment, and our consequent use of our cities, schools and homes. The way in which we act upon our environment and perceive the consequences of our actions may be crucial to our survival as a species. The area of environmental psychology is therefore a fitting growth point.

Psychology and the Environment belongs to Unit F of *Essential Psychology*. What unifies the books in this unit is the concept of change, not only in people but also in psychology. Both the theory and the practice of the subject are changing fast. The assumptions underlying the different theoretical frameworks are being revealed and questioned. New basic assumptions are being advocated, and consequently new frameworks constructed. One example is the theoretical framework of 'mental illness': the assumptions of normality and abnormality are being questioned, together with the notions of 'the cause', 'the cure' and 'the doctor–patient relationship'. As a result, different frameworks are developing, and different professional practices gradually being initiated. There are, though, various social and political structures which tend to

7

inhibit the translation of changing theory into changing practice.

One interesting change is the current aversion to theoretical frameworks which liken human beings to something else. For example, among many psychologists the analogy of the human being as a computer which characterizes Unit A is in less favour than the concepts of development (Unit C) and the person (Unit D).

Essential Psychology as a whole is designed to reflect this changing structure and function of psychology. The authors are both academics and professionals, and their aim has been to introduce the most important concepts in their areas to beginning students. They have tried to do so clearly but have not attempted to conceal the fact that concepts that now appear central to their work may soon be peripheral. In other words, they have presented psychology as a developing set of views of man not as a body of received truth. Readers are not intended to study the whole series in order to 'master the basics'. Rather, since different people may wish to use different theoretical frameworks for their own purposes, the series has been designed so that each title stands on its own. But it is possible that if the reader has read no psychology before, he will enjoy individual books more if he has read the introductions (A1, B1, etc.) to the units to which they belong. Readers of the units concerned with applications of psychology (E, F) may benefit from reading all the introductions.

A word about references in the text to the work of other writers – e.g. 'Smith (1974)'. These occur where the author feels he must acknowledge an important concept or some crucial evidence by name. The book or article referred to will be listed in the References (which double as Name Index) at the back of the book. The reader is invited to consult these sources if he wishes to explore topics further.

We hope you enjoy psychology.

Peter Herriot

8

1
Background and beginnings

Environmental psychology is concerned with the scientific study of man's relationship to his environment.

Expressed so briefly, this definition has a gradiose, all-encompassing ring about it – and some psychologists have understandably been moved to ask politely whether it does not stake out the greater part of the discipline. Far from it, of course. The difficulty is that the word *environment* represents a very large and imprecise concept. It was adopted ready-made into Middle English from a French word 'environ' meaning to form a ring round, surround, encircle; as with a number of other importations from France, we added the suffix '-ment' to express the result or product of the verb so that 'environment' now means that which 'environs', especially the 'conditions or influences under which any person lives or is developed' (OED).

This is indeed comprehensive. Unfortunately we lack a suitable set of words for narrowing it down or splitting it up. There is certainly no single word or qualifier which sufficiently conveys the limited field of environmental psychology. This is concerned, for example, primarily with the *physical* environment and only with the social environment in so far as the two are connected; however, they are intimately connected in many environmental settings. It is not limited to the built environment, but includes the natural; both these might be covered by the words 'geographical environment', but we would wish to include also the critical spaces immediately surrounding the person, i.e. the 'body image' and the 'body buffer zone'. In fact, it is more informative to say that environmental psychology is concerned with all the various concepts that man has devised to represent space; with studying man's *responses* to the patterns of *stimuli* that people experience if they selectively move about in the intervals which lie between objects, desired or aversive.

The mention of 'stimuli' and 'responses', concepts which have come under some suspicion in recent years, prompts a further elaboration of our definition. Man does not have a passive, one-way relationship with the built or natural environment. He is an active, striving, seeking organism who can both select and modify his own milieu (see F7). At whatever phase of this circularity one breaks in, it is predictable that the most potent influences upon man and man's most powerful influences upon the environment will be found to be mediated through those physical features which in turn control social behaviour.

Notwithstanding the interactive nature of man's relationship with the physical environment, much research in environmental psychology has been conducted to inform *policy decisions* and for this purpose has tended to concentrate on one direction of the interaction, i.e. the effect of the environment on man. The adoption of 'environmental determinism' in this sense is merely a sensible expedient. This is an issue that will be discussed at greater length in a later section, but an early warning is needed that the use of this research strategy should not be taken to imply that environmental psychologists see man as a helpless puppet.

To return to our definition, environmental psychology is distinguishable from the traditional fields of perception because most of the stimuli that the latter has dealt with, though issuing from the physical environment, have been abstracted from it and impinged upon captive subjects in the controlled condition of the laboratory (see A5). Indeed, they have frequently been two-dimensional representations of the environment and not the environmental objects or forms themselves. This is a very proper procedure for scientists and it has taught us a lot about the characteristics of stimuli and the ways people respond to them; but very little about the environment – which is a higher order, structured organization of stimuli.

There have been exceptions, and a notable one is distance perception, which might very well have been regarded naturally as belonging to environmental psychology if it had developed in a different era.

Experiencing the environment through sensation and perception leaves a residue of knowledge or of 'cognitions' in the central nervous system. We might say that the person is never quite the same at any successive moment in time and, indeed, it is mainly the processing of sensations in the context of these stored experiences that renders them into human experiences or perceptions. Hence, cognitions or 'learnings and thinkings' about the physical environment are also included in our subject, but again, much traditional learning theory is at a quite different level of analysis (see A3).

Add to this the fact that many of our experiences within the physical environment are 'affectively toned', giving rise to emotions and beliefs, feelings, attitudes, judgements and values, and it can be seen that the field is indeed a broad one on the response side, although not so all-encompassing as our initial definition suggested on the stimulus side.

Architecture and planning – the 'client professions'

What about the 'client professions' – those architects and planners who might ultimately benefit from any advances in our understanding of the environment? They have to be discussed separately because although many planners started life as architects, the opposite is not the case and the two professions have quite different styles.

Architecture

Architecture is a 'noble art' by tradition. Its origins are close to painting and sculpture and its great exponents in the past served aristocratic patrons and built exclusively monumental buildings. However, some would wish to distinguish 'architecture' from 'building' in the same way that 'poetry' is set apart from 'verse', but the analogy holds if we claim that building is the all-inclusive concept, that all buildings have to be designed or 'architected' and sometimes the results are poetic and at other times prosaic. 'Vernacular architecture'

11

still comprises the larger part of the built environment and this was an unconsidered by-product of construction, whether carried out by a builder or by the intending occupier himself.

The traditional ethos of architecture as a profession has been the Beaux Arts, and although there is a yawning gulf between Inigo Jones and the modern entrepreneural architect – who may control a partnership employing nearly 1,000 men and be vastly more familiar with the committee room and the computer print-out than with the drawing board – the basic sources of inspiration are still the same. They are nurtured most particularly in the training schools, where there is great emphasis on creative originality and still a system in which students are required to produce a progression of complete design projects which are then presented for the subjective, global evaluation of their tutors in 'crits'.

Practice, of course, is a hard, pragmatic and intensely complex business (one has only to try thinking oneself *in advance* through every successively integrated step in building a garden shed, let alone a hospital, to realize this), but its apotheosis as distinct from its 'bread and butter' is ultimately as a *visual art*, i.e. what the building will look like. Every true-blooded architect nurtures images of the competition cathedral or opera house deep in his psyche. The 'school' and 'practice' sectors of the profession tend to be at odds with each other – but to the outsider this looks like a case of ambivalence in both camps!

One consequence of the Beaux Arts tradition is that, unlike many modern professions, architecture has for long been bereft of an established research tradition to back it up. This is changing now, and building science and other support disciplines are making rapid strides although, regrettably, their principal concern remains with the behaviour of materials and not that of occupants. This is not to say that a balance should be attained by reducing the technological research, but rather that there should be an increase in human science research.

It has been pointed out by James Scott, a research-oriented housing architect, that we still lack anything that could be called a sophisticated analysis of the human and social criteria that even the ordinary house is intended to achieve, either in its internal or external ramifications. Once these criteria are established, we are still faced with the task of assessing the

12

potential of different physical forms for achieving them. Canter (1970) expresses the dilemma nicely when he says 'no coherent framework has been developed which presents both the building and the user in the same picture'.

If these observations seem exaggerated, there is a simple way of quantifying them. It is open to anyone to make a quick survey of the literature of architecture by walking through a suitable library. It would be surprising if he could point out one book in a hundred that expounded on the ordinary human use (as distinct from the objective professional evaluation) of past architectural creations. Perin (1970) has gone further to make a full content analysis of the transcriptions of jury evidence for a major architectural award: 'in looking for theory of human nature that might be expressed in the vernacular of people whose main work is architecture, I have read the Progressive Architecture Magazine Award jury comments for the past eight years. I cannot find any; I find as a matter of fact so few words in that language that describe or identify "human beings" or "human needs" that I have to conclude that the basis of judgement did not include any such category.' She also refers to a study made by Hassid who found that from a total of no less than forty-five separate criteria which were used to judge architectural work for award purposes, only two were concerned with the extent to which the needs of the human being were fulfilled in the design. These criteria, furthermore, were underemployed by comparison with others.

It might be argued that so far I have drawn a caricature of architecture. If this means that the distinctive features have been emphasized, the charge is fair. It is true that the 'functionalist' movement advocating that form should *follow* function, has produced great changes in emphasis. But looked at another way, it is surely ironical that such a declamation should be necessary. Perhaps the reason is that, although the functionalist view is widely accepted, it has been possible in the curiously complex jungle of ambivalences, conflicts, prejudices and bland equivocations that characterize every profession, for architecture to take functionalism on board while still cherishing the pre-eminence of art.

These considerations are partly reflected in the method used within the profession for the mutual evaluation or appraisal of its products. One source of the growing rift between

13

the profession and the public can perhaps be partly attributed to the fact that traditional appraisal machinery is somewhat inbred. The public may comment and complain (and not infrequently does) but it is the judgement of colleagues that gives the architect his kicks, in both senses of that word.

The method itself is the dissemination of drawings and, more recently, of glossy photographs and slides, showing in the majority of cases the external elevations of buildings. People are occasionally depicted, but their main *raison d'être* is to convey 'scale'. They are not normally shown to be *using* the buildings. Interiors are not often illustrated and verbal assessments of the way in which the building 'works' are comparatively rare. Systematic scientific appraisals of the human 'fit' are almost non existent.

Having said so much, we must hasten to repeat that the picture is changing rapidly. The innovative style of the architect makes him more receptive to new ideas than most, and environmental psychology is being eagerly embraced. This is happening at a time of very rapid change, in which the architect has found himself, for the first time, not in undisputed sole command of design projects but as one profession among many whose collaboration is essential to the creation of a new environment. For example, more than half the cost of a modern hospital is devoted to technical services. The architect's agonizing professional decision is whether to bid for the leadership of the team or to break into a controlled number of formal specialisms under the RIBA (Royal Institute of British Architects) umbrella, each of whom might be recognized. The spread of skills involved is too broad for him to cover the whole spectrum under one membership category for very much longer.

The planning professions

The planner is a different animal altogether, and the differences are not merely attributable to the fact that he operates at the macroscale of the environment. Although many are now trained 'ab initio', the majority in practice had an apprenticeship in one of the established social sciences such as geography, politics, economics, law or sociology — each of which has a strong research tradition and no more than average interest in the arts. Instead, in a sense, they might almost be said to belong among the 'caring' professions – if it is appropriate to talk of 'caring' for communities and societies.

Planners have a much stronger research tradition than architects but in common with other 'applied professions', such as education, their research methodologies draw mainly on their back-up disciplines, although a distinctive research approach is beginning to emerge. From the psychologist's viewpoint, there is some cause for regret that the majority of their methods are 'objective', based on observations of derived statistical data, and that the 'phenomenal' or subjective approach, through the ways in which ordinary people perceive or respond to their environment, is hardly represented. Psychologists have plenty of bitter experience of the frustrations of attempting to predict human responses directly from the environment without considering the mediating variables, i.e. the 'person' in between.

There is, of course, a strong element of environmental conservation (a desire to preserve our heritage) in planning and this is the way in which its aestheticism is expressed. This has somehow to be integrated (not 'compromised', a word which has overtones of defeatism) with a large number of other variables; most notably, with economic values and the 'get up and go', 'make a clean start' values that usually go with them.

Planners have a stronger belief than architects in environmental determinism; the philosophy that peoples' lives can be influenced by planned decisions about the environment. This is understandable, not only because they might be said to be wielding larger units, but because they are disposing these units in relation to each other and hence controlling priorities. Objectives seem closer to the surface in planning and hence it is the author's view that psychology has as much or more to offer at the planning scale than at the architectural, and should find communication easier, both for this reason and because of a more closely shared research orientation.

So far these hopes have not been realized and relatively less interest has been shown. There is not far to go in seeking explanations. One is that all planning problems are so perplexingly multidimensional. Decisions at the end of the day often have to be made 'holistically' or intuitively and implemented by protracted and subtle processes of negotiation and political manoeuvre that are not enlightened by much contemporary

15

research. A second, less obvious, reason is that the practitioners already have their established research procedures, and although there is some degree of overlap with psychology there are undoubtedly boundaries which it is not only laborious to cross, because of the unfamiliarity involved, but also 'career attenuating', because of the implications of detachment from one's 'in-group'.

A historical sketch of environmental psychology

The history of our subject is a brief one. Although scattered papers throughout the present century could be said, in retrospect, to belong within the field, it did not begin to develop a collective consciousness until the 1960s. An early milestone in the United States was the Salt Lake City conference on Architectural Psychology and Psychiatry, held in 1961. In Britain, the first of several symposia on the subject was held at the Annual Conference of the British Psychological Society at Reading in 1963. The Building Research Station (now the Building Research Establishment) employed at least one psychlogist during the 1950s and this involvement expanded during the 1960s, which also saw the rise of the Pilkington Building Research Unit at Liverpool University and the Building Performance Research Unit at Strathclyde University.

The first significant conference in Britain was held at Dalandhui (Strathclyde University), Scotland, in 1965; and this has been followed by similar occasions at Kingston Polytechnic, 1971, the University of Surrey, 1973, and at the University of Sheffield, 1975. In the United States the large-scale interdisciplinary conferences sponsored by the Environmental Design Research Association (EDRA) form an important series.

The whole scholarly apparatus of symposia, conferences, journals, books, newsletters and, more recently, abstracts has been established in a surprisingly short time and there is intense and rapidly growing interest in many countries. Universities in the United States have followed the lead of the City University of New York and the University of Utah in establishing graduate programmes and a vast proliferation of courses. In this country, a one year postgraduate course in

16

environmental psychology was established at the University of Surrey in 1973, and an increasing number of undergraduate courses include some treatment of the subject. There is a burgeoning interest in Europe (particularly in Scandinavia where two international conferences have been held at Lund), and also in Japan.

Much of the impetus has come from outside establishment psychology, notably from the design professions. Although this may account for the present lack of scientific rigour and coherence, it should also be said that on the credit side its unquestionable intellectual vitality and excitement can be attributed to its multidisciplinary origins, with contributions from geography, planning, ergonomics, political science, biology, anthropology, sociology and engineering.

Although there are relatively few psychologists who would claim environmental psychology to be their primary research activity, there is considerable interest within the profession, and this has been recognized by the inclusion of a chapter in the illustrious archives of the Annual Review of Psychology (Craik, 1973) and by the setting up of a Task Force by the American Psychological Association.

The species and sub species of environmental psychologist

To understand the species 'environmental psychologist', the first point to make is that the label derives from what he actually does and not from his university degree. There is, however, a certain social awkwardness about this because academics, in particular, are passionately devoted to their native discipline and generally prefer to belong to a subsection of that, calling themselves 'behavioural geographer' or 'environmental sociologist' for example, than to take out citizenship papers for a new mixed state.

This chauvinism could well be used to explain why psychologists want their colleagues from other disciplines to be labelled environmental psychologists: Touché! But there is a further ambivalence here, because their colleagues mustn't then presume to think this entitles them to be called 'psychologists'. This is a different matter altogether, involving the most stringent professional qualification requirements!

Labels should not be allowed to create silly demarcations, but on the other hand it is just not true to say they don't matter. They strengthen identity and steer the direction of effort.

The second point is that the field is characterized by various 'modes of approach' at what might be called the professional practice and academic levels. It is helpful to distinguish (a) building appraisal (or system evaluation); (b) ergonomics (or compatibility studies); and (c) scientific theory building. Any single environmental psychologist may be involved in all these at different times and they merge into each other. However, they do have different aims and ground rules and much confusion could be avoided if both client and customer were aware which game was being played, as it were.

Building appraisal
Building appraisal is oriented to the single building, the 'one off'. It is based on the notion of feedback, a basic mechanism studied by psychologists and taken over from mechanical engineers. The perfection of even the simplest human action depends on the return of information about what happened last time. This feedback has two main effects; it forms the basis for correction of errors and it generates the rewards and punishments that motivate further action. The second of these two effects is easily overlooked if engineering systems are taken too slavishly as the model, unless, of course, one includes the operator in the system. A blind man playing darts by himself would not only show zero improvement in performance of the task but would quickly become bored. The provision of a sighted scorer to give instantaneous feedback by moving into a position adjacent to the dart board immediately following his own turn (the established ritual of the art) helps enormously.

One hesitates to point the analogy to the architect because, of course, he is far from blind and he has his own methods of appraisal (see Ch. 3). But it is hard to escape the conclusion that, say, the disadvantages of the tower block as a family residence might have been less persistent if better feedback mechanisms had existed, or if these had not been based on limited criteria, such as visual impact or land use economics, and a limited audience which excluded the ordinary user.

Appraisal, then, is a procedure for providing information about a single building when it is in use. It is to be hoped that the environmental psychologist will be in partnership with

18

architects in establishing criteria of satisfactory functioning and methods of measurement to gauge the extent to which these criteria are realized. It can be compared to the clinical method in psychology, where the orientation is first and foremost to an individual patient – but, as with the clinical method, building appraisal merges into other 'modes of approach' as the lessons learned from every building are, or should be, accumulative. The aim is not to usurp, and certainly not to devalue, the function of the brilliant and gifted designer. It is rather to preserve, analyse and transmit some of his secrets so that a higher proportion of the next generation will emulate his skills.

Ergonomics or compatability studies
Here we are once again concerned with cutting cakes in a variety of different ways. But there is no need to apologize, as this process of 'categorization' is the whole basis of active perception and cognition. It only causes trouble if we delude ourselves that there is some ultimately accurate set of subdivisions of 'reality' instead of sets which are more or less helpful for different purposes.

Ergonomics is a fairly new alliance of the members of established disciplines such as engineering, biology, psychology, and physiology. They are committed to exploring the man-machine interface. The 'fit' between man's dimensions and capabilities and the machines he contrives to achieve his ends. In so far as a simple hand tool, a chair or a house is regarded as a machine, environmental psychology could be regarded (and is by some) as a branch of ergonomics. In our view, ergonomics is a branch of environmental psychology, for two reasons. The first is that the orientation of ergonomics is to practical man-machine systems, e.g. man/car, man/crane, man/altimeter, whereas environmental psychology extends more widely to include more *relational* concepts such as personal space, crowding, privacy, belonging, isolation etc. The second reason is that ergonomics is properly concerned with compatibility, normally leading to design recommendations that will make the environment work more smoothly with or for people. A detailed example is given in Chapter 4 of an ergonomic study of housewives working in the kitchen leading to design recommendations on sinks and work-top positions

19

and dimensions. Other studies have been done on the best height for baths and water closets. Environmental psychology should normally extend further than compatibility to the design of environments that will induce *change* in people. This view is not shared by all and considered outrageous by some, but it will be explained more fully later.

Again it is necessary to emphasize that ergonomic studies merge into our next category, scientific theory building. This is because some criteria of compatibility are so all-pervasive, with relatively consistent results across a variety of man-environment situations, that they lend themselves to theoretical generalization. Good examples are thermal comfort and lighting efficiency; and to a lesser extent, the response to traffic noise and even to what is called 'visual intrusion' (i.e. the blocking of people's view or outlook) in the evaluation of the urban landscape. Once these environmental processes are understood sufficiently to name them as parameters and to model them, the borderland has been crossed into theory.

Scientific theory building

The desperate urgency of emphasizing and explaining the distinctiveness of this approach arises from a need to bridge the deep gulf of understanding that tends to separate the hard-headed, hard-working, pragmatic practitioner who actually has to get on and make decisions, to build offices or schools or to plan motorways (on which the nation's survival wholly depends) and the dreamy, taxpayer supported, unrealistic, over holidayed, slow moving, non-deadline-meeting academic (on whom nothing of real consequence depends).

These are mutual stereotypes and as such, recognizable as absurd caricatures. But very real differences do exist and it is only if each extreme can reconstrue the other that their roles can be made constructively complementary. It is true that many psychologists in the past have been exceedingly prone to contrive theoretical sculptures from artifical abstractions and to seek most of their rewards from displaying these structures to other psychologists or to even more hallowed members of the scientific community. In the interests of 'control' they have abstracted stimuli to the point of emasculation and presented them under laboratory conditions with inevitably gross distortion but in ways that make for the speedy production of scientific papers.

Having said this, the whole history of science says loud and clear that the biggest advances have rarely been made by attempting to solve everyday practical problems but by pursuing leads towards underlying lawfulness. Hence there are very strong grounds of expediency for insisting that not all psychologists should try to be expedient all the time. A balance must be established. It is no use insisting that every advance should be translated into simple language for the delectation of the ubiquitous layman, because many scientists can't do it at all, others think it would be wasting their scarce research time.

A common source of frustration for the practitioner is that theoretical generalizations in the human sciences often have a self evident ring; 'discovery' is rarely dramatic. This is usually because both positive and negative forms have already been heavily confirmed from lay experience ('too many cooks spoil the broth'; 'many hands make light work') and it is only the laborious elucidation of the detailed circumstances in which each of these generalizations holds that yields advance in understanding.

For example (and continuing our analogy!) it would be simple and extremely useful to *discover* a threshold point above which human beings experience overcrowding. But no such threshold exists. Reality takes a more complex form. The first task of the theoretician is to devise a skeleton framework of concepts (including the ways in which the main 'bones' interact) and to see if it works when compared with the real world. Altman (1975) offers such a framework, covering one extensive area of environmental responding. *Privacy*, he claims, is an optimum level of interpersonal activity (not simply a retreat mechanism) based on an individual ideal which in turn depends on situation and personality. *Crowding* is the experience of an excess of activity beyond this level and *isolation* or loneliness is a shortfall. It remains (though Altman and others have begun the task) to define and explore the manifold influences of personality, situation and type of activity. Only then will the practitioner be able to make predictions for the real world.

Hence, although a unified theory would ultimately have practical value, the subtle point is that its application should not determine the priorities in its construction. These should be set by the need to fit together the many unconnected bits into a coherent system, capable of bearing and integrating the load of later additions without basic redesign of its foundations. It follows that knowledge which binds and connects and has the effect of organizing and composing will often be given higher value by the scientist, although it may appear remote and useless to the man of action.

A quote from an earlier article seems apposite here:

> There is a tendency for architects to expect design applicability. Similar frustration is doubtless experienced by general practitioners in medicine when they observe from their crowded consulting rooms the remote, 'self justifying' activities of the academic *physiologist*. At times, it is true, early results of theoretical research may imply no more than a set of instructions to grandmothers on how to suck eggs. However, despite their protestations, it is surprising how inept some grandmothers are at this task. New vistas may open for them as statements of the obvious become consciously formulated in their minds for the first time. There may even be additional bonuses as these statements link across to transparent truths in previously unrelated areas of their activity. (Lee, 1971)

Environmental determinism

There is one final distinguishing characteristic of environmental psychologists that deserves a mention. It concerns their commitment or otherwise to what might be called the philosophical position of environmental determinism.

Most scientists proceed on the fundamental assumption that natural events have causes, or at least antecedents. This notion is called scientific determinism or, when it is applied to the environment, environmental determinism.

To identify the causes of phenomena is regarded as one of our most powerful forms of explanation, but when these phenomena are *human*, the notion becomes troublesome and contentious. The reasons appear to be that it implies firstly the negation of free will; secondly a passive, one-way moulding of people by environment and, thirdly, that the environment is the exclusive agency that totally shapes behaviour. In fact, none of these conclusions is a valid deduction from environmental determinism and much of the dispute would be resolved by semantic clarification.

For example, if the indeterminist wishes to aver that his choices are free, and if by this he means that no external environmental forces are governing his choices but that only he is responsible for them – then he is at the same time admitting (indeed, claiming) that he determines his choices. We must then look further to see what innate or acquired forces shape the qualities of character that enable him to do so.

What will be asserted in the pages that follow is simply that the physical environment is one of the sets of influences bearing upon behaviour, judgements, perceptions and emotions. To this extent, it partly shapes our personalities. Conversely, we have powerful forces at our command to shape the physical environment. Hence, at both an individual and governmental level insofar as we learn to understand the consequences of man-environment interaction we shall be more capable of shaping our own destiny. The present limitation is our ignorance.

2
Theories and Concepts

While it is accurate to say that all environmental psychologists have common cause in seeking the understanding of man–environment interaction, it certainly cannot be claimed that they share the same ideas about how to get there or about what kind of model to use.

Most of the well known theoretical systems, with their attendant methods of enquiry, have been applied and we will try to parade these dispassionately before introducing our own candidate.

The purpose of a theory is to build a symbolic representation of 'reality' that will explain it. First, one must categorize the phenomena of the natural environment into units that are judiciously selected or designed to facilitate subsequent stages. What is meant here is that if we were trying to 'explain' the internal combustion engine, the optimal units would probably be the cylinder block, crankshaft, magneto etc. and no amount of painstaking attention and conceptualization of the oil filler cap or the fan belt would advance matters so rapidly. Best of all, of course, the abstract relational concept of 'explosion' would be a break through.

Secondly, the units are represented in symbolic form by the use of words, numbers or physical objects. *Definitions* link the abstract concepts (which are chosen for their ease of handling) to their real world equivalents. Next, the interconnections between concepts are either averred by simply observing the real world (induction) or by postulating links first and deliberately testing them against the real world in observation or experiment (deduction). The connecting pattern that gradually emerges between concepts can be expressed either in mathematics, in graphics, in three dimensional models or as is usual in the human sciences, by connected prose.

The difference between different kinds of psychological theory are rarely different ways of attributing the same phenomena to different causes. More usually they deal with different levels of human responding, use different-sized units, advocate different ways of observing them and, most important, deal with different content areas. Freud wrote almost nothing about the intellect and Piaget has written even less about the emotions (see C1 and C2).

Theories

The influence of theory on environmental psychology is helpfully considered at two levels. First, there are the broad theoretical positions that have had a pervasive influence on the thinking of all psychologists, such as psychoanalysis (see D3), gestalt (A4) and behaviourism (A3). At the next level are narrower theories that have been more specifically applied as frameworks for environmental research, such as Barker's ecological psychology and Kelly's personal construct theory (F1).

Psychoanalysis

It is often claimed that Freud's system is a theory of instincts, but if this implies the remorseless unfolding of particular patterns of behaviour it is a false picture. Certainly he postulates an energy force driving the person from within, the libido, which at the beginning achieves consummation only through sensual pleasure. But his whole emphasis is on the progressive *differentiation* of the 'id' (the reservoir of libidinous drives, needs, thoughts and plans) and in particular the splitting off of two major and partially autonomous departments, the ego (conscious self) and the super ego (the internalized morality of family and society). These deal with the real world. The differentiation and the articulation of the personality is shaped by interaction with the environment. In psychoanalysis, the

25

environment means mainly the crucial social context of family relationships. These determine the balance of libidinal development, the environmental objects which give pleasure and the distribution of gratification between different objects. But although social relationships are at the roots of this process, the 'reality principle' (i.e. inevitable constraints on immediate gratification) means that libido cannot continue to be attached to the self and the family and is forced to generalize to other people and to inanimate environmental objects.

These positive and negative feelings, depending on their social acceptability or utility, may exist as part of the conscious ego or the unconscious id. In either case, they determine our behaviour. Freud put considerable emphasis also on the fact that the growth and maintenance of such systems is a turbulent affair and there is much intra-psychic conflict. This is more important to clinicians, yet psychoanalysis would claim also that the conflicts are reflected in the value systems of a society – and hence in its symbols, artefacts and built environment.

Social relationships between people are reflected in their spatial interaction and this would be one obvious area of application of psychoanalysis. For example, the libido has to be progressively transferred from attachment to the mother (initially to the breast) to attachment to the world at large and to opposite sex objects. This process is literally a spatial separation as well as an abstract social one and although it can be effected smoothly in the context of a family house, garden and neighbourhood, evidence suggests that the path is less smooth if the family live in a tower block or if the child is removed to an institutional setting.

There has been little direct application of psychoanalytic ideas in environmental psychology, but an exception was a brilliant pioneer paper by Charles Madge (1951) in which he pointed to the high importance in the planning function of distinguishing private from public space and suggested how residents of housing estates have models of behaviour deriving from early childhood experiences. For example, the house symbolizes the mother's body and is a protective shell separating the familiar from the unfamiliar. The confidence which the child acquires in moving from the mother is reflected in the ease with which the resident moves between the home and neighbourhood, or his withdrawal into protected isolation. The repression of sensory pleasure in the mother's body is reflected in the extent to which the resident may suppress aesthetic pleasure in the external appearance of houses in the use of colour, decoration and so on. He also claimed that the garden may serve as a transitional social–physical space where the 'libido flows through the garden to the outside world'. The community centre, corner shop and pub may furnish significant social roles that meet the unexpressed needs established early in family life.

It is easy to smile at the more exotic suggestions of the psychoanalyst, but they have a way of enduring and, after all, many of them need only to be reformulated in terms of stimulus generalization and secondary reinforcement to earn greater acceptability. However, they would still need to be empirically verified. Perhaps some intrepid environmental psychologist will one day explore the rich storehouse of unconscious perception and desires about *place* through dreams or free association.

Gestalt psychology

It is not unfair to describe gestalt psychology as a 'movement' because it was born during the 1920s and 1930s from an almost revolutionary attempt to shift the whole direction of psychology from two existing trends. The first was associationism or structuralism, the attempt to discover (through trained introspectionists) the irreducible molecules of cognition and sensation. The second was psychophysics, in which the search was for lawful relationships between external stimuli and experienced sensation. The former has been overthrown, but the latter has retained a valuable niche, albeit more by virtue of its method and applicability to certain real life problems than because of its original theoretical base.

The term 'gestalt' does not translate readily from the German, but it means 'whole' or 'configuration'. The most important dictum is that 'the whole is more than the sum of its parts'. The effect of the movement has been to embolden psychologists to conceptualize and analyse molar and meaningful units instead of pursuing a false reductionism in the belief that this is 'real science'. Also, the gestaltists have, from their primary concern with perceptual processes, strengthened the

27

approach of 'phenomenalism' (i.e. attempting to understand behaviour from the individual's world *as it is perceived*) and established the foundations of a range of cognitive psychologies.

Finally, gestaltists have stressed a synchrony between the stimulus forms of the external world and neurological processing mechanisms in the human perceiver. This gives rise to strong innate tendencies to perceive stimuli in certain ways. 'Figure' stands out from 'ground'; complex arrays form themselves spontaneously into groups, incomplete figures are under tension to 'closure'; existing continuity tends to extend itself. These 'laws of organization' of the perceived environment have stood the test of time and seem particularly apt to our appreciation of townscape and scenery. They can, however, be deduced from a functional theory (i.e. we learn to organize our spaces in these ways because it pays off) and the gestalt notion of neuro-physiological correspondence is not now generally accepted.

Kurt Lewin (1936) was a gestaltist who extended into social psychology this basic orientation of phenomenalism, the use of molar units and the notion of dynamic interaction within a field of forces. Lewin introduced the concept of the individual's 'life space', containing inner representations of external objects endowed with positive or negative valence (liking or disliking) by personality or situational factors. The life space is the 'situation as perceived' and it contains a variety of barriers (abstract or real) varying in their permeability, which separate the self from the goal region. Behaviour is represented as 'locomotion towards the goal' within this dynamic set of forces.

These concepts have had considerable influence on social psychology but neither Lewin himself nor his followers made much direct use of the framework or of the topological mathematics proposed for its analysis, in their own research. This was partly due, no doubt, to Lewin's untimely death. But it could also be argued that the problems of (a) how to (or whether to) aggregate the life spaces of different individuals in order to derive generalizations about human behaviour and of (b) how to represent the *organized combination* of different individual life spaces that must comprise interacting social groups, were not resolved. They both remain an intractable problem for any theory of environmental psychology, as for social psychology generally.

Behaviourism

Behaviourism is the most widespread and familiar of theoretical systems in psychology. It too began as a revolt against introspectionism and mentalism and with the aspiration of replacing their woolly harvest with good hard scientific facts. With this aim, only directly observable and hence measurable behaviour was to be admissible evidence. While J. B. Watson is generally credited with paternity, the theory could not have advanced very far except upon the foundations laid by Pavlov through the discovery of the conditioned response. In this basic S-R linkage, the natural reflexive stimulus was shown to be replaceable by pairing (in successive presentations) by a new, initially irrelevant stimulus. The behaviourists saw this form of 'classical' conditioning as the mechanism by which to explain the rapid and extensive ramification and diversification of behaviour that originates from a few natural reflexes. The environment, both social and physical, provides the stimuli and is therefore the shaper of the large majority of behavioural responses.

It was a difficulty that laboratory attempts to establish conditioned responses in humans proved more capricious, to say the least, than Pavlov's use of harnessed and salivating dogs. However, considerable impetus was given to the theory when a Cambridge psychologist (Grindley, 1932) showed that an initial, 'reflex' stimulus to elicit the response before pairing begins is, as it were, no more than a convenient option. In his paradigm, one simply waited until a guinea pig turned his head to the left and then allowed it to nibble some carrot. If it turned right, as it sometimes did, no carrot was supplied. This type of learning, confirmed by a number of other investigators, was later called operant conditioning. It is much more characteristic of human behaviour than the classical CR. Responses that operate on the environment to yield rewarding consequences become established and repeated. Many thousands of animal and human experiments attest to the reality of this principle. More recently, applications such as token economies (systematic rewarding procedures for shaping the behaviour of subnormals in institutions) and behaviour therapies for the 'unlearning' of phobias or behaviour deviations have demonstrated the validity of the mechanism (see A3).

There is, however, surprisingly widespread distaste for behaviourism (see F8). The grounds are that it undermines the notion of free will and carries the dangerous threat of manipulation by Big Brother. Skinner, the acknowledged doyen of behaviourism, claims that these fears are unfounded and that any disadvantages are outweighed by the potential benefits. He deploys some powerful rational arguments, but these seem merely to confirm the fears and to inflame further the passions of the opposition.

The most explicit statement on the application of stimulus response theory to design has come from Studer (1969). He suggests that the environment can be analysed as a prosthetic phenomenon, in two distinct but inter-related modes; i.e. it maintains physiological drive states and hence the *goals* of behaviour and it is *behaviourally prosthetic*, '... in that it intentionally configures specific behavioural typographies'. The problem for the designer is summarized in the following quote (the language is ponderous but not untypical):

Let us look at the nature of the interface problem. A desired behavioral state (R2) has been specified. The participants have not been previously emitting this particular system of behaviors but another (R1) (otherwise no environmental problem would exist). It is desired that they will. They have quite diverse, generally unspecified behavioral histories, and the problem is one of specifying an environmental configuration which will produce, with the highest probability, the specified state of behavioral events. What this clearly describes is a *learning* situation, i.e. the acquisition of, or modification toward, a new system of behaviors.

Direct applications of this approach are rare. They are found mainly in the control of therapeutic environments. Again, however, its effect on research is pervasive, leading, for example, to the selection of behaviour as the most favoured level of analysis. Also to the choice of relatively small behaviour units (e.g. 'Anne licked her finger: she turned to the correct page') and of direct observation, which is preferred to reported measures of behaviour such as questionnaires and interviews. It should not be thought, however, that the converse applies and that the adoption of these methods necessarily implies the use of S–R theory.

Barker's ecological psychology

For about twenty-five years, Roger Barker (1968) has been leading a team of researchers at the Midwest Psychological Field Station in Oskaloosa, Kansas, who have intensively studied 'Midwest' itself and other communities in USA and England. It could be claimed that Barker has developed one of very few theories that are directly concerned with environment. Others would suggest that it hardly constitutes a *theory* in the conventional sense.

It comprises the systematic and detailed observation of what Barker calls the 'stream of behaviour', which is made up of 'behaviour settings'. These are recurring patterns of activity (the participants are interchangeable) that take place in a particular locale. Careful sampling methods are used to ensure that the full range of settings representative of a given community are studied. They may include settings such as concerts, political meetings, supermarkets, bridge parties, playgrounds, buses and so on. Detailed observational records are made of each setting by an observer who samples in thirty minute blocks and writes down all the behaviour episodes against a time base. The result is a highly detailed profile of the community.

While he and his students are not opposed to prediction and explanation in the sense of relating antecedents to consequences, they claim that we must first carry out the long overdue task of building clear and detailed pictures of what actually happens in everyday life. The model is essentially a socio-spatial one. If a person 'inhabits' (not merely enters) a behaviour setting, he will behave in accordance with the explicit set of rules that are apposite to that setting. This is conformity but it is not *uniformity* because settings require complementary and hence different actions from the people involved if they are to function.

An important concept is that of undermanning/over-manning of behaviour settings. This is used in an exhaustive study comparing large with small schools (ibid.) The latter have less variety of settings but on average each setting is undermanned (because there is a scarcity of children to play the different roles) so more children are actually drawn into social activity; and each individual child experiences a wider range of settings. This study represents a shift from the largely descriptive approach of the behaviour ecologists to a more explanatory mode.

Kelly's personal construct theory (PCT)

It is earnestly hoped that the basic philosophy underlying Kelly's theory has already been manifested in the preceding pages. This is the view that there is no such thing as absolute truth or objective reality but only a range of alternative ways of construing events. This is not to say that all 'construct systems' are of equal value, for some are more effective than others in achieving comprehension and in predicting future happenings. The first of Kelly's formally stated fundamental postulates is that 'a person's processes are psychologically channellized by the ways in which he anticipates events' (Kelly, 1955).

It follows that our attempts to devise theories of man-environment interaction are no more than a professional intensification of something that everyone is doing all the time. This is precisely Kelly's view, which he makes explicit by saying, not that scientists are human, but that man is a scientist. Hence the theory is *reflexive*, instead of allowing psychologists the indulgence of adopting one model to explain other people's behaviour and a different model to explain their own activity in doing so, the two are one and the same.

The theory is obviously a cognitive theory, but it is important to emphasize that constructs are not merely 'perceptions' but 'perceived anticipants'. If we construe a person as 'friendly', we do so because we perceive him as someone who on some future occasion will act in a neighbourly way, will refrain from speaking ill of ourselves and may respond more positively than others to a request for a small loan.

The total system of a person's constructs is his personality. The purpose of analysis is to describe its hierarchical structure. Constructs may be superordinate or subordinate, narrow or wide in their 'range of convenience' (application), 'core' or peripheral, and the whole system may be complex or simple, 'tight' (high correlation between constructs) or 'loose'. For example,

'Domestic' is a superordinate construct which over-arches 'cottagy', 'Georgian', 'suburban semi' etc. The construct 'cosy' may be used by some people quite widely to describe anything from a dugout to a penthouse suite; others would reserve it for cottages. A core construct is one that is close to the self; for example, 'chintzy' may be construed as 'like me' or 'unlike me'. Some people construe the built environment in simple terms, i.e. using only a few exclusive categories, whereas others have complex interrelated construct systems with many branches; for example public buildings might be divided not only by function but by such subtle distinctions as Roman, Classical and Palladian. A loose construct system is more flexible, speculative and open ended in its predictions. The effect of the 'stylish–homespun' construct is looser in its predictions than one dealing with room temperature.

As with all theories in psychology, there is an implied methodology which is all too often adopted for the purposes of ardent fact gathering while the theory itself gets scant attention. In this case the method is the Role Construct Repertory Test (Rep. Grid) (see D3, F1) and its purpose is to obtain a model of a selected area of a person's construct system. One of its strengths is that the constructs should first be *elicited* from the subject rather than imposed by the investigator, and there are several alternative ways for doing this. The method of triads, for example, begins with sets of three elements, e.g. study, lounge, kitchen. The subject is then asked how two of these elements are the same but different from the third. This may yield the constructs brittle, chintzy, sterile, sociable etc. The constructs are then arranged in a 'grid' by means of which the subject can be asked to assess the relevance of all constructs to all elements. Recent multidimensional scaling methods and the use of computers have rapidly accelerated the analysis of grids.

It was Stringer (1970) who, in a milestone paper delivered at the Dalandhui Conference, introduced Kelly's theory to architectural psychologists. His exhortation was not restricted to its value for research. He stressed the advantages for both psychologists and architects of adopting the flexible 'constructive alternativism' advocated by Kelly. This attempt to 're-construe' the world in ever new ways would help in mutual understanding and it would also deliver them from the mere attempt to reproduce the environment of the past. 'Instead of merely designing so as to preserve the particularities of men he has observed, [the architect] can design so that (men) re-construe the world, change and become new men.'

Stringer (1974) has recently demonstrated the potential of the PCT approach in the study of the ways in which a range of alternative plans for the re-development of a shopping area, (the elements) are variously construed by housewives. Sub-groups of different ages, length of residence, shopping habits and car ownership were compared. The study fits into the cur-rently important context of public participation in planning. The measures Stringer derived relate both to the structure of people's construct systems and to the actual nature of their constructs. He addresses what is perhaps the most difficult dilemma presented by the theory; i.e. that if constructs are to be truly *personal* the results from groups of subjects cannot easily or meaningfully be aggregated, but it is precisely this that we often need for testing hypotheses (see A8). He shows that elicited constructs can be grouped into categories by like-mindedness (language is a public activity) and these categories (as distinct from the idiosyncratic constructs) can then be taken as the items of analysis.

There are obviously considerable strengths in PCT theory but it is at an early stage of development. There is little evi-dence so far on the correspondence that exists between peoples' construing of the environment and their overt behavioural interaction with it. It might also be questioned that the whole of environmental cognition is encoded linguistically or in forms for which the subject can readily supply linguistic equi-valents. Not all our images have names.

Socio-spatial schema

My own theoretical approach evolved from a study of urban neighbourhood carried out in the early 1950s (Lee, 1954). There was some doubt at that time whether the neighbour-hood still existed as a salient feature of life in the city and if so, whether it should be defined as a social group or as a piece of territory. In seeking an answer to these questions, an inductive empirical approach was taken. Ordinary people were asked directly whether they possessed a neighbourhood or not and if so, what it was like. It was found that the respondents neither could, nor wished to, distinguish the physical from the social relationships they had within the local environment; most of them had formed an organized synthesis of the two, an inner structure which was functionally very important to the ways in which they perceived and used the city. These findings led to the formulation of the 'neighbourhood in the mind' and later, to the use of the concept of the *socio-spatial schema* to represent this and the numerous other 'inner representations' or images of the environment that the normally mobile person possesses. Methodologically, the main problem becomes one of how to elicit these schemata without distorting them in the process.

The concept of schema was originally used by Sir Henry Head, a distinguished neurologist, to describe the neural patterns that must be progressively built in the cortex to tell us where our limbs are. He was particularly intrigued by the 'phantom limb' phenomenon whereby a limb seems to its owner to be present long after it has in fact been amputated. It was Bartlett (1932), however, who made the greatest contribution by applying the schema in his classic attempt to explain the processes of remembering. He reacted against the notion of stimulus-response 'connectionism', which implied the accretion of molecular memory traces which would be weak or strong, long-lasting or short-lived, as a function of their individual natural histories and particularly of their association with reward. In place of this, he stressed the active, constructive processes of memorizing and recalling. Schemata are modified by the selective assimilation of inputs which are relevant or appropriate to them and once this has occurred, the input is dead, finished. Schemata themselves are dynamic, that is, they change in order to incorporate new material and this material itself changes them further; but they are selective in what they incorporate.

It is a common experience that we build spatial schemata of different parts of the city and that the new discovery of a particular road which links two sections, emerging at a particular angle, can suddenly transform the whole orientation and scale of our perception.

Psychologists have been almost totally preoccupied with schemata of physical objects – that is with the ways in which people endow objects with meaning (see A7). They have neg-

35

lected schemata of space. Yet information about the 'whatness' of objects is virtually useless without information about their 'whereness'. Objects cannot be pursued as goals unless we have some idea where they are. For this very good reason we store, in coded form, a spatial location for every class of objects known to us. Just as everything must be some*thing*, so it must also be some*where*. It is virtually impossible to conceive of an object that does not have some kind of spatial coding. It is generally very surprising to find objects in the 'wrong' place; imagine a large pink blancmange resting on a hatrack or an octopus reclining on an escalator!

There is ample evidence that structure is the principle by which large quantities of coded information can be stored (see A6) and this is as true of spatial as of object information. Much of our spatial conceptual information is best stored by the use of verbal labels, such as 'up–down', 'high–low', 'near–far'. Many of our own socio-spatial schemata on the other hand, are pictorial type representations such as the body image, house, neighbourhood, city, country etc. They exist in nested form, i.e. one within another; each contains distinctive parts that have become articulated in high detail and others that are vague (see Ch. 7). They are personal, unique and dynamic.

These schemata are essential to navigation. Navigation is essential to mobility. We have to form plans to make future journeys, whether to reach out an arm to pluck an apple or to embark on a safari across Africa. Plans may be verbalized but more often they are constructed, for spatial mobility purposes, by evoking intermittent images of the destination and of points on the route. It is like running a set of pictures past a window in the mind. Given the plan, we initiate action, but at intervals it is necessary to check the reality against the image and to interpose necessary corrections when we find ourselves off course. The end of the plan is the arrival at a destination.

In predicting a person's likelihood of embarking on a journey, his schema provides better data than any measures of the real environment. This is the argument for a phenomenal or subjective approach to environmental psychology. Many of the mediating variables (i.e. influences such as age, sex, social role) that have to be entered into the prediction equation are incorporated in the schema.

The affective, or aesthetic, aspects of environmental responding can be handled within the theory by saying that part of the assimilated set of meanings that comprises every socio-spatial schema is its affective quality, its positive or negative valence.

Finally, it should be re-emphasized that a socio-spatial schema is an inner representation of both physical and social objects in an integrated form. Thus, social structures are isomorphic (i.e. take the same or similar form) as spatial structures. The relationships between judge, prisoner and jury within court proceedings are reflected in the layout of the court room; between crowd and football players in the design of the stadium; between teacher and pupils in the design of the school. Navigation within social structures ('getting ahead', 'moving closer together', 'sitting on the fence') is similar to navigation within physical structures and can be planned in the same way by the generation of images or verbal representations of the present and of some projected future state.

Concepts

The whole range of psychological concepts are variously deployed in environmental psychology, but there are three that are almost unique to it. These are privacy, personal space and territoriality. Each has been defined in a variety of ways and used in theories. Regrettably, most of these theories are little more than classifications or typologies.

Privacy

Much of the confusion over privacy would be removed if it were recognized that the phenomenon itself can be studied at various levels, perceptual, cognitive or behavioural, without changing its nature. A person may, in the same situation, be studied as one who perceives, knows, seems, feels or acts in ways that could be said to lie at some point along a dimension from extreme over-privacy to extreme under-privacy.

Some authors stress the 'rights' to privacy, others the set of control mechanisms for maintaining it and others the relief from social pressures endowed by it. While emphasizing again that the choice of concept is a matter of scientific expediency and not a search for the golden fleece, we are forced by the demands of brevity to offer a 'best buy'. Hence, it is proposed that privacy is most usefully defined as 'a condition of *optimal* access by others to the self (or group)'. This definition does not prejudge the level at which the 'condition' may be measured, but it meshes particularly well with the concept of socio-spatial schema. Such a schema will be experienced as, for example, satisfactory, pleasurable or comfortable, unless it is characterized by too much (or too little) of the *appropriate* form of social interactions. It is important to stress that unwelcome behaviour by a few people may have the same intrusive quality as less offensive behaviour by a larger number. A few people trampling over one's flower beds may seem just about as disturbing to privacy as hordes of people peering over the garden wall.

As in the cognitive structuring of all plans for action, it is possible to generate an 'ideal schema' and to take a series of control actions to change an existing schema into an ideal one. We have a whole stock of these ideal schemata for different occasions, such as making love, having a few friends in, travelling in a rail compartment, taking a picnic into the country. They vary in spatial size and in their social structure. Their boundary permeability (i.e. the ease with which people are 'allowed' by us to gain access to the self) is extremely varied. However, we don't rely entirely on a portfolio of ideal schemata or we should be unable to orient ourselves or to 'feel right' in completely new situations.

There are various means of privacy regulation at our disposal. At the behavioural level we can act overtly to prevent trespass into successive layers of our personal space (schema), the area surrounding the self which moves about with us. If people intrude into our privacy by staring, for example, we can 'stare them out' or turn the body sideways; if they touch us in a way or on a part of the body that is not pleasurable (or, if pleasurable, nonetheless unwelcome!) we can take evasive action or administer an admonitory slap. If the invasion is threatened to a fixed territory, such as a selected group of arm chairs in an old persons home or a military club, we can station representatives of the ingroup to scarecrow intruders, or place personal objects (markers) to signify ownership. It should be re-emphasized, however, that both personal space and territory regulation may comprise behaviour designed either to repel social interaction or to incite it. The latter tactics will be used where privacy is so great as to incur feelings of loneliness. Also, the regulation can be effected not only by bodily communication but by all forms of verbal communication, e.g. 'we really should get together more', 'whatever made *you* come?' These are techniques (in the short term) or plans (in the longer term) to change the boundary size, composition and social structure of socio-spatial schemata.

Finally, what constitutes an optimum level of privacy and an acceptable set of regulating mechanisms is strongly determined by social norms. We acquire our schemata not only by direct functional relationships with the environment but by conformity processes within society. For example, the norms about undressing and semi-nudity are different on the beach from in the office. Again, middle class people often talk loudly and ostentatiously on buses and trains, working class people usually prefer the privacy of *sotto voce*.

Personal space

Every person has an area of space surrounding the body, the boundaries of which exist only 'in the mind' and into which any intrusion by others is unwelcome; an invasion of privacy. The space itself is not necessarily circular. In fact, there is good evidence that it extends furthest in front and least at the sides. Edward Hall, an anthropolgist who wrote a book in 1966 entitled *The Hidden Dimension*, has been most influential in establishing the concept. He proposed a new science of 'proxemics', the study of ways in which space is used as a form of communication. However, Hall's observations, which related mainly to cultural differences, were almost entirely qualitative and, to some extent, speculative. It is Robert Sommer who, in a series of experiments and observations has demonstrated empirically the relevance of the concept to environmental psychology.

Hall distinguished four spatial zones used in social interaction; intimate (0–18 inches), personal ($1\frac{1}{2}$–4 ft), social (4–12 ft), and public (12–25 ft). These zones are obviously influcnced not only by the kinds of actions we wish to perform but by the range of our senses, i.e. the length of our arms and the distance that our voices will carry without undue exertion.

However, they have the shortcoming of most typologies, i.e. they oversimplify what are actually a multiplicity of *continuous* dimensions. In fact it is a main feature of the application of the concept of personal space that most of its manifestations are *learned* and thus highly varied between different cultural and other groups. Also that the number of personal spaces is almost as numerous as a person's patterns of interaction. One investigator (Jourard, 1966) counted the number of body contacts per hour between couples in cafes in different countries. The highest was 180 (San Juan, Puerto Pico) and the lowest 0 (London). He also found there were differences within cultures in who touches whom and on what parts of the body.

It nonetheless remains useful to classify normative or individual personal spaces but they should be cross-classified by situation (physical or social) and they then become equivalent to socio-spatial schemata. Otherwise, we may find ourselves uttering unhelpful tautologies like the following, taken from an otherwise excellent source: 'Studies of close contact between friends support the idea that very close distances are appropriate for people in an intimate relationship' (Altman, 1975).

Territorial behaviour
There has long been a distinction drawn by psychologists between 'ego-centred' and 'domi-centred' spatial systems. Very young babies, it is believed, perceive the world as literally revolving around themselves. Their earliest spatial coordinates radiate like spokes outwards from themselves at the hub, so that all distance and direction estimates are self-other based.

However, this system is quite soon supplemented (though not wholly replaced) by a revolutionary change in orientation. The environment is perceived as static and the self as moving through it. This is obviously more efficient for interacting with other people, but it is important to realize that the sensory input remains identical. Only the interpretation differs. It is at first similar to the experience of sitting in a just-moving railway carriage and looking at the people in the stationary carriages of another train as one draws out of the station. It often takes a couple of seconds to realize that it is oneself that is moving and the other train that is still. It is possible to perceive and predict the outcome of movement when it occurs both in oneself and other persons simultaneously, but this only becomes feasible because we learn to take our frame of reference from the static elements in the environment. To pursue the train analogy, we discover what is 'really' happening if we can see the platform or some other fixed reference.

Of course, although the 'domicile' is the first and always a very important fixed reference, it is later supplemented by many more general landmarks. As Oliver Wendell Holmes once said, 'The axis of the earth sticks out visibly through the centre of each and every town or city'.

This domicentrism coexists with egocentrism. Although we use an object-object frame of reference a great deal, we also perceive a space surrounding the self at centre that is mobile with respect to the static world; a self-object frame of reference. This perspective is, of course, the 'personal space' discussed in the last section. *Territory* is a structuring of *static* space (through which personal space moves) for which a person feels some possessiveness.

Many students of animal behaviour, particularly Hediger (1950) have indicated the very powerful role of territoriality in the life of birds, fishes, primates and other species (see D2). It is also universally acknowledged that human beings show possessiveness about their 'den', 'turf', 'beat', 'office' or almost any demarcated piece of environment. As with certain species of primate, even nomadic behaviour is not immune from the effect. Territories are set up temporarily and then abandoned, as with the encampments of gipsies or with the reservation of spaces in railway carriages.

Attempts have been made to explain human territorial behaviour, and particularly aggressiveness, by claiming that it is instinctive. The argument goes as follows. Since humans have evolved from primates, they retain vestigial traces of those instincts which are of basic biological significance. Since aggression is functionally part of the innate territorial defence pattern of animals, human aggressiveness is also instinctive and linked to territoriality. Just as animals 'mark' their territory by urinating, by depositing glandular secretions or by issuing recognizable vocal signals, it is said that humans use markers such as fences, 'keep-out' signs or deposit articles such as hats, or copies of *The Times*, to indicate temporary possession.

41

However, there are substantial differences. Animals are frequently forced to subsist wholly in one territory within which all their nutritional and nesting material needs are met. The area also has to act as a preserve for marital relationships. Its size appears to reflect a balance between a pre-programmed disposition and the plenitude of supplies in the particular environment.

Depending on the species, much of the territorial defensive behaviour is ritualized and does not have to be learned. It is evoked by species-specific signals. For example, one ethologist showed how the male robin will attack a piece of red rag, red on the breast being the critical aspect of an invading male robin. An intruder who does not display this signal, however realistic in other respects, is not molested.

Human beings are very different. They move freely between large numbers of overlapping territories, use a limitless number of culturally learned markers and appear to recognize invasions by cues of great subtlety and abstractness and to respond to these functionally rather than automatically. The student, for example, has a home territory, often with a garden gate and a front door, beyond which is the more intimate territorial sanctuary of his bedroom. Each space has its threshold of privacy. He would resist or resent invasion with differing degrees of strength using a variety of techniques of which aggression is only one; he might also use verbal hints to indicate a desire for solitude or the withholding of hospitality signals.

When he travels to university, he may establish territory on the train, possibly resisting invasion of the neighbouring seat (unless the carriage is crowded) by 'marking' it with a guitar or similar baggage. On arrival, he enters a campus territory, passing a janitor who, with the help of a gate or various signboards, filters a selective entry. He then proceeds to a study bedroom where his unique territorial rights are recognized by his possession of a key.

Hence, it would seem more parsimonious to say that territoriality is acquired and extensively ramified from the basis that space has enormous utility for human beings. Some degree of space is an essential prerequisite for every human activity and it becomes a precious commodity with a currency value depending on its supply. In most environments, some of it has to be shared and elaborate social systems are therefore contrived to allow this. The differences from animals are so great that it seems more profitable to concentrate on the ways in which territoriality in humans is culturally learned. One prominent ethologist has argued that the mode of acquisition is immaterial. But if this is so, we are left with little more than an analogy – a low level of explanation. More so, it can be argued that the origin makes a great deal of difference in one sense because, broadly speaking, if the forms of territorial behaviour in humans were innate, they would be ineradicable. If they are learned, they could be changed in this generation or the next by the adoption of the philosophy that man is an active autonomous agent who can shape his own future (see F7).

3
Method and measurement in appraisal and research

The present chapter is included because the methodology of environmental psychology does, in many ways, present unique problems. Also because the field is an interdisciplinary one and a review of methods is likely to be particularly useful to non-psychologists. It includes, as an appendix, a compendium of measurement techniques that are of common application to appraisal, observation and experiment. The balance of treatment in the text, however, reflects the already excellent coverage of some areas, such as experimental design, elsewhere (see A8) and gives more space to strategies and techniques of appraisal.

There are three principal methods used in environmental psychology, building appraisal, observation and experiment. These parallel other fields of psychology if we equate appraisal to the 'clinical' method (see F3). What these two have in common is that their orientation is to the single case and research is not their first objective. In the clinical method, the first duty of the psychologist is to the patient. In appraisal, the primary task is to assess the functional effectiveness of a particular building. In both cases, the data may be collated for their relevance to theory as well as practice, but this is secondary and optional.

'Appraisal' is a modern-sounding word, but as a concept it is as old as architecture. Indeed, a substantial portion of the literature of the profession is devoted to the recording of drawings and models, and more recently of glossy photographs and slides, for the deliberate purpose of exposing the works of architects to others (though mainly to colleagues) in a process of mutual evaluation or appraisal. The use of competitions for individual buildings and the award of institutional prizes is another manifestation of the same process and it can also be seen in one of its most ritualized forms in the 'crit' system which prevails in schools of architecture.

However, a large portion of this traditional appraisal has been restricted to judgements on a single though complex criterion – the aesthetic satisfaction which the exterior architectural form gives to the spectator. No one would deny the importance of this, but in recent years there has developed some healthy turbulence in the profession as it has tried to ride the storms created by an exploding science and technology. The Functionalist movement, mentioned in Chapter 1, shifted the order of precedence for aesthetics over function that had prevailed in the Beaux Arts tradition, and declared that form should *follow* function. This injunction is now widely accepted, but architecture has managed to take functionalism on board while still cherishing the pre-eminence of Art. Although the schools devote much of their design criticism to whether a building will 'work', one suspects that the highest prizes in the profession are reserved for those who show 'creativity', 'originality', 'spontaneity' and similar qualities. It is still true to say that the proportion of photographs of the exterior elevations of buildings reproduced in the journals greatly exceeds that of the interiors. Furthermore, although the textual material of evaluations (which is voluminous) now makes reference to how the building may be expected to 'function', it is rare to see any objective assessment of human response by the people actually using it.

Of course there is also a kind of appraisal that is akin to natural evolution. If a building works it feels comfortable and looks right and, as with a good pair of shoes, people go on using it and may even enquire who designed it – especially if they are thinking of buying another. Unfortunately, this survival-of-the-fittest mechanism does not make much contribution to the refinement of the design process because buildings all survive too long – even the bad ones – and always seem to be in short supply. Other professions have an advantage here. Surgeons can be appraised by whether or not their patients die and lawyers by whether or not they win their cases because the tempo of feedback is more rapid.

However, enough has been said of the traditional methods to demonstrate that the concept is not new but that the existing techniques are inadequate to the scale and speed of today's operations. What of the new developments?

It is the emergent partnership between architecture and the behavioural sciences that has given a sudden self-consciousness to appraisal. In almost every sphere, society has discovered the benefits of monitoring its own on-going activities and using the resultant information to govern decision making. The best methods of monitoring have been found to be those developed by scientists, originally for the extension of knowledge in a more fundamental sense. Architects are late starters in making use of this, and scientific appraisal is still only an experimental and tentative part of its procedures. No trace of it, for example, has crept into the formal costing and contracting aspects of building construction. The newly developing tendency is part of a much wider change in the philosophy and modus operandi of architecture as a profession, which is increasingly conscious that the primary purpose of the large majority of buildings is to provide a framework for human behaviour as well as a stimulus to its associated emotions. It has been reflected in at least one important symposium devoted to the subject in the United States and by the sponsorship, in Britain, of two long-term research units, the Pilkington Research Unit at Liverpool University and the Building Performance Research Unit at Strathclyde University.

If appraisal is to be more widely adopted by the architectural profession, the form it will take needs to be written in at the briefing stage. It is here, after all, that the objectives of the building (as well as its physical specification) should be agreed and it is against these objectives that it should later be judged.

The adoption of criteria for appraisal

It follows from the argument developed throughout this book that every building has a set of purposes that can be defined in terms of *human behaviour*. This is often regarded as implicit, not worth spelling out or writing down. There is an exact parallel in a totally different field of psychology, i.e., that of employment selection and assessment (see E2). A new, say, Works Manager, is needed and his purpose and duties in the organization are thought to be so well known that advertisement can proceed without further ado. The management selection consultants ('head hunters') who have prospered so well in recent years have done so by showing the enormous value of writing a detailed and clear brief (to use the architect's equivalent concept) couched in terms of long- and short-term human behaviour.

The process should be one of *negotiation* to which the architect (and hopefully in the future, his behavioural scientist colleague) makes a considerable contribution from his knowledge of environmental psychology. The customer alone cannot be expected to have the skills to analyse the behaviour patterns and values of his organization – whether it is an insurance company, a church congregation or a family. His very familiarity may well be an obstacle.

The briefing should lead to the establishment of *criteria* against which the success of the building will subsequently be measured. It is important to realize that the criteria in appraisal studies are *indices* which are selected on two main grounds. Firstly, they must represent without bias (or serve as accurate samples of) a large range of complex behaviour that is itself way beyond our powers of direct observation. Secondly, they must be readily measurable.

Again, an analogy to what is called the *validation* of personnel selection procedures is helpful. One of the criteria by which packers in a porcelain factory might be appraised is the number of breakages in a given period. This would scarcely do for the sales manager, for whom the main criterion would obviously be the volume of orders. In both cases, however, the criterion is an easily measurable but essentially representative index. It would be impossible in either case to record and measure the whole functioning range of work activity. If more than one criterion can be measured, the aim will be to choose them so that the most important areas of behaviour are sampled.

Incidentally, the word 'appraisal' has overtones that are benign, soft, aesthetic, almost optional. The substitution of the word 'validation' might suggest a stronger, moral obligation on the architect to test his creations against reality and to learn from successes and mistakes, to eschew what Wools (1970) has called the 'cuckoo mentality' in which buildings are laid like the eggs of that irresponsible bird and then hopefully abandoned.

The broad strategy of appraisal

The broad strategy of appraisal must inevitably be comparative because there are no anchors, no absolute standards. There is no way of determining, for example, 'normal' human convenience or the 'right' amount of effort to expend in moving oneself upstairs. One solution is to establish norms. This is done by measuring the average and distribution of the responses in a given population and then to compare our observations with these comparative standards. Canter (1974) for example, has taken judgements from a range of schools and of teachers to form such a basis of comparison for educational buildings and from doctors and nurses for hospitals. There is a close analogy with the measurement of intelligent behaviour (see D4). The norms can be expressed in a variety of ways, some of them very simple, but they depend ideally on the collection of data from a representative sample, and so far this has not been attained for any building type.

Other strategies are a) to take measurements before and after people have occupied a building, or b) to compare the rehoused occupiers with a sample of people who are similar in all basic respects except that they have not been moved into a new building. The difficulty with the former alternative is that people are *slow to adapt*, by which time other factors are likely to have changed. With the latter, the problem is the 'Hawthorne effect' – people who are rehoused are often gratified by the implicit goodwill of the gesture and likely to respond warmly to questionnaires, distorting their true feelings for the building.

Methods of building appraisal

It is mainly the *strategy* of building appraisal that is different from other forms of applied environmental psychology. The methods may be any chosen from the full range available for measuring responses (although they would normally be among the simpler, quicker ones) and their detailed discussion is therefore covered by the sections that follow. Only one or two general comments are appropriate here.

It is pertinent to ask what distinguishes scientific observation from the casual observations of the layman, and this is very important to appraisal because most existing procedures are more like case studies – the sort of thing that any intelligent and perceptive observer with a tidy mind could do. The answer is that there are no clear boundaries. The scientific method differs in degree only – on a number of dimensions. For example, the observations must be unobtrusive, free of bias, accurately recorded and representative. The achievement of these objectives at even a reasonable level is beyond the layman unless the behaviour is very simple indeed. Many instruments have been developed to make things easier. Some of these are obvious devices, such as tape recorders which ensure accuracy of the data, but what is not always understood by the architect is that the data itself, once collected, is totally unmanageable unless it can be processed using software instruments such as percentages, matrices, correlations and factor analysis to expose its essential characteristics.

The other distinguishing feature of the scientific method is the exchange of observations in the interests of verification and comparison (see A8). The activity is essentially cumulative but the accumulation has to be somehow both orderly and flexible. Although there is a place for the 'one off' appraisal study, it is to be hoped that its results will eventually be communicated through journals or lodged in a data bank and hence used again.

Levels of human responding

Human responses to the environment, like all responses, are sequential and interdependent (see A4). Behaviour does not occur without some perception of the situation. The energy emissions from the environment are processed in the central nervous system by the structured residue of past experiences, by present moods and by genetically determined predispositions. The perception that results is unique. It is *accompanied* by feelings or emotions which are partially determined by it. This complex may then be expressed in behaviour. Both the perceptions and the behaviour leave further trace effects on the store of organized experience, and hence have an influence on subsequent perceptions, feelings and behaviour. Because of the prodigious time capacity of human memory, behaviour may be influenced by perceptions occurring many years previously (see A6).

The environmental psychologist has to make a decision on which stage of this cycle he will try to monitor. Shall it be the emotions the subject feels or the perceptions he experiences as he looks at or smells or listens to the building? Shall it be the organized system of 'knowings' that has been formed as a result of transactions with the building? Shall it be the behaviour itself as it occurs? There are two further alternatives, both 'packages'. We can attempt to measure the unique ways in which he 'construes' the building. How he is programmed by his past experience to perceive and act towards it. This is similar to his 'attitude', although the latter is a much broader concept and often, but not necessarily, polarized on the single dimension favourable/unfavourable (see B3). However, it is a convenient point at which to break into the cycle because it is an organized synthesis of feelings, cognitions and motivations that predispose us to behaviour. The diffuse behaviour to which it predisposes may take months or years to express itself and its *direct* observation may be virtually impossible.

It is important to realize that all these processes are consistently inter-related and there is much to be gained from observing at more than one level as a check on reliability. For example, in a study of the effects of urban motorways on residential communities (Lee, Tagg and Abbott, 1975) the investigators measured cognitive maps, the frequency of 'trips' made by people across the major road, inclusion of local landmarks in the neighbourhood, knowledge of local landmarks and expressions of attitude towards the neighbourhood. These showed an encouraging correspondence, though least for the measures of local knowledge. It seems that the neighbourhood that one 'belongs to' is different from the area that one 'knows'.

The choice of response level will also be determined partly

by the hypotheses or problems being explored. A church or an art gallery is obviously strongly intended to evoke emotion. For the designer of a shopping precinct, actual purchasing behaviour may be paramount and the designer of an industrial or office building may consider that favourable employee attitudes is the most important outcome.

Frequently the sheer economics of research are overriding. This is one reason why the marvellously compact verbal scales are so often used and why the reactions of university students are the most heavily researched!

If behaviour is measured directly, the task is formidable because the detail is so great, and if indices are selected as a short cut, there is always a risk that they do not represent the total pattern. When measuring emotions, the technical difficulties of direct observation using physiological recording are considerable and it is much easier and often just as valid to ask people how they feel.

Yet another determinant in the choice is the degree to which the act of observing is likely to distort what is being observed (see F7, F8). People become introspective and self-conscious if too obviously watched or if asked to 'answer some questions'. Among many complications, they ask themselves what their response 'ought' to be and tend to 'fake good'. Psychologists have devised ways of minimizing these effects but they often invoke fresh, if smaller, problems. Unobtrusive behaviour recording raises ethical questions; the disguise of attitude measures can be effected by the use of projective techniques (by which an ambiguous stimulus such as an ink blot, an uncompleted story or a vague photograph, is used to elicit responses which are thought to reflect differences in subjects' personalities), but they make recording more difficult and interpretation more equivocal (see D3).

Observation and experiment compared

An experiment is essentially a contrived situation (see A8, A9, F8). Something is deliberately changed with the express object of seeing what happens in consequence. The experimenter starts with some idea about what is likely to happen (called a hypothesis) and finishes up with some evidence on how good an idea it was in the first place. In some cases, the results may throw up a better idea. *Observation*, which may be 'naturalistic' or 'controlled', is used to collect information about what happens in normal situations where there is no deliberate change introduced by the investigator.

It is sometimes mistakenly supposed that the only really 'scientific' method is the experiment. This is patently not the case. If it were we would have to blackball astronomy, geology and a number of other eminently scientific disciplines. Experiments are frequently impossible especially in the human sciences. But there is another, more subtly mistaken notion that experiments are *always best* providing they are feasible. On the contrary, the great virtue of the method is that it enables us to make more confident statements about the *causality* of events – and by the same token it is the greatest shortcoming of observational studies that causality (as distinct from the 'concomitance' established by, for example, the statistical method of correlation) is very difficult to establish.

Conversely, however, there is a considerable virtue which the method of observation can claim, and one that is particularly important to environmental psychology. It is easier to control the distortions that occur from the intrusion of the investigator into the situation. The disturbing effect of an 'audience' is not only to arouse people to unnatural levels of motivation, it also changes their forms of behaviour. Observation conserves reality.

Why is it difficult to establish causality from observations? It is because this method can only document the existence of relationships between events (correlation) and although this is a *necessary* condition for inferring causality, it is not a *sufficient* one. It could merely mean that the two variables are both related to a third one and have nothing directly to do with each other.

For example, it may be found that the mean intelligence level of nursery school children is correlated (inversely) with the size of schools they attend and it would be easy to infer (especially if one were a committed environmental determinist) that the size and layout of school buildings is the cause of the difference in performance. However, it is well established that there are substantial differences in the IQ of children from homes of differing social classes (see C1), and if these children are also more likely to be allocated to large schools there need be no causal link at all between the building and the children's intelligence, however accurately the data are gathered and correlated.

However, it is another common misconception (especially in 'survey' research) that absolutely no causal inference can be drawn from observational research. In fact, by using 'cross-breaks' and other analytical procedures it is often possible to test alternative causal explanations and by eliminating them, to strengthen the postulated one. For example, in one study (Lee, 1963) an hypothesis was set up that almost anyone can be induced to join a social club, simply by reducing his energy costs by situating the club building nearer to his home. This was contrasted with the notion that people are inveterately either 'joiners' or 'non-joiners'. The main finding was a high correlation between density (and hence proximity) of clubs and the probability of joining. However, where there is a high density of clubs there is also a high density of old people, of working class people, and of longer term residents. It is these who might have been the true cause of the correlation. Hence the data had to be sub-divided by each variable to see if proximity and use of clubs are correlated, for example, *both* for young people and for old people, for middle and for working class people and for long and short term residents. In this case, the original hypothesis remained intact.

Conversely it must always be remembered that an experiment gives no guarantee of the validity of a causal inference; this is secured only if the experimenter has identified and successfully controlled all the possible interfering variables. This is a very difficult thing to achieve.

The final point to make in comparison is that the techniques of measuring human responses to the environment are the same whether one is engaged in an observational study or 'observing' the consequences of an experimental manipulation.

Observation

The term *naturalistic observation* is usefully employed for the on-site observation of real life situations, involving minimal or nil disturbance; whereas controlled observation is used for situations that are stage managed by the researcher under conditions that make observation easier. This distinction is described in more detail later, and the points to be made in the following sections apply to both forms.

The need for unobtrusiveness

Obtrusiveness most obviously occurs when *behaviour* is being directly recorded. The psychologist has devised many ways of minimizing it, such as being around so much that the novelty of his presence wears off, carrying out a role within the organization (participant observation), collecting sensitive information while ostensibly taking some socially neutral measurements, using concealed recording devices, observing through one-way screens etc. Some uses of these are constrained by ethical considerations and each situation is so different that it is hard to draw clear boundaries beyond which the ends no longer justify the means. Two general remarks are relevant. If people are in a 'public' space they generally accept that they are liable to be observed and the distinction between casual and systematic scrutiny is not one that causes too much offence. In, say, semi-private institutional settings much of the ethical difficulty can be removed by seeking general advanced approval. Although there may be initial self-consciousness, this dissipates quite quickly.

A less obvious form of obtrusiveness occurs when measurements are taken of people, not when they are actually behaving, but before or after, i.e. when asking them to describe past behaviour, to anticipate future behaviour or to describe perceptions, attitudes, feelings or emotions that they have expressed or would be likely to express in a given environment. In all these cases, the facts that the situation is not real and that the questions are asked by a person with a peculiar role and status, may distort the answers. This problem is sometimes referred to as the 'reactivity' of measurement procedures. Again, there are many ways of reducing it, only a few of which can be mentioned here. Being aware of its dangers is an essential start.

Most techniques for reducing reactivity can be considered as various ways of disguising or withholding from the subject the purpose of the measurement. Again, there are ethical problems (see F8), but these can often be overcome by pointing out to subjects that disclosure would bias the results and promising to explain fully afterwards.

Another method, used all too infrequently, is to discuss the problem of reactivity with the subjects in a frank and level-headed way, and to enlist his cooperation in overcoming it. This can be done best in a face to face situation but the same principle can be extended to the written instructions that precede a questionnaire or test.

The representativeness of observations

Representativeness is fundamental to all research. The whole point of observing (or experimenting, for that matter) in a particular situation is in order to generalize to similar situations on a much wider scale, whether temporal or spatial (see A8). All observations, in this sense, are samples drawn from a universe of possible observations. If they are not representative of this universe the results cannot be generalized to it. One of the most common malpractices is to first study a sample and then wonder how far or to what universe the results apply. This is standing the procedure on its head. These strictures do not apply to appraisal, of course, where the intention to generalize is of low priority; but this is precisely what marks appraisal as different from research and why some students who intend to do research finish up with no more than a limited appraisal of some situation.

True representativeness is, of course, a counsel of perfection but one that should always be aimed for. The best route is through random choice. This is not often possible, and the next best alternatives may be exemplified from social survey methods where accurate sampling is a high priority. The method of *stratification* means that the main subgroups of the universe (e.g. sex, social class etc.) are identified and then the samples are taken from each of these and the results added together. *Multi-stage sampling* is also extremely useful. When the universe is widely scattered, samples can be drawn from large units, such as electoral wards, and then a sample of polling districts drawn from within this subset until finally a sample of people is drawn from the subset of polling districts.

Even at the most primitive level of representativeness, when the choice of sample units is very small, it helps to choose units that are 'typical'. Hence the choice of 'Midwest', 'Plainville' and 'Midland city', for sociological community studies. It needs to be noted that the representativeness of a sample is not a function simply of its size, but also of the degree of variation in the parent universe and of the amount of error that can be tolerated. A sample of twenty houses for example, would probably be more representative of all houses in Britain than a sample of forty schools would be of all schools, despite the big difference in the size of the respective universes.

Units of response

One of the traditional debates in psychology has been over the units of behaviour that should be studied (see A1). The polarity is between those who record fractional elements in the interests of accuracy, confident that mathematics (or later research!) can synthesize the data into unitary wholes; and those who feel that behaviour is only meaningful if recorded in wholes because these involve much more than the sum of their parts. Researchers of the latter persuasion approve such terms as 'molar' and 'global' and this level of categorization has now shown itself to be reasonably dependable, overcoming earlier misgivings. It was Lewin, an early pioneer of social psychology, who asserted boldly that if we could not trust ourselves to recognize the meaning of coherent sequences of behaviour, ordinary social life would have proved impossible.

For environmental psychologists, the observations and labelling of global units of behaviour is probably made mandatory by the demands of economy. It is relatively cheap, for example, to classify the readers in a library as engaged in (a) serious study, (b) random browsing, (c) non-studious work, (d) day dreaming, or (e) miscellaneous other. It is much more expensive to take time-lapse photographic records of postures. It is doubtful if there would be any advantage.

There is an important point before we leave this polarity, however. The accurate recording of some fractional piece of behaviour that may in a sense seem trivial can be an extremely valuable technique if it has been selected as an index of more complex operating. For example, the frequency of head movements during a sample of lectures might well be taken to represent the levels of concentration and interest maintained by the audience. The same principle often applies when a more abstract concept has to be measured for theoretical reasons.

For example, Mehrabian and Russell (1974), consider 'arousal' to be a primary concept for environmental psychology and this can be measured, for example, by heart rate, facial expression or speech volume.

Time, space and event sampling
In spite of a plethora of modern recording aids, the observation and analysis of significant periods of human behaviour is extremely laborious.

Time sampling is one way of reducing this unmanageable burden. Recordings are made only at intervals. If these intervals are randomly distributed over time the sample of behaviour is also random and hence representative of the whole. It is usually more practical to make observations, say, every hour and this yields a 'systematic' as distinct from a random sample. This will be adequately representative providing care is taken to overcome 'periodicity' in the events to be recorded. For example, in a hospital, the issue of drugs and the taking of temperatures occurs at prescribed intervals and could be missed altogether or be quite disproportionately represented. A related difficulty is that authorities understandably try to restrict observation to the less busy periods, and if this has to be conceded the investigator should make it clearer than he usually does that his generalizations apply only to part of the universe of activity.

Exactly the same principles are applicable to *spatial sampling*. Instead of drawing a sample of times in order to generalize about the behaviour that occurs in a particular place, we may wish to sample behaviour throughout a given building or housing estate. It is as impossible to be everywhere as it is to be anywhere all of the time. The equivalent to the systematic sample is the choice of intersection points on a superimposed grid. A random sample in space can be drawn by assigning numbers to systematically distributed points and then selecting a sample from random number tables. Alternatively, the population can be stratified in terms of spatial units, such as private rooms, corridors and public rooms or types of person, such as males and females, doctors, nurses and patients, so that these can be sampled more accurately. One of the great advantages of stratification is that one or more strata can be sampled with smaller sampling intervals, i.e. to produce more subjects. This is done when there is a particular 'domain of interest' (e.g. female doctors) for which one needs a larger subsample for adequate study. When generalizations are to be made about the total universe, the data for these strata are re-weighted appropriately before being added in. This useful principle applies to both time and space sampling. In observing behaviour in a student residence, for example, a sampling interval of one in ten rooms might yield enough individual student rooms but not of bathrooms, so these would be sampled with an interval of one in two. In such a study in which I was once involved, it became clear that the important social groupings were reflected in the choices made by students of which bathroom to use.

Event sampling has not been much used in environmental psychology. Instead of attempting to record and then to categorize all behaviour in a given time or place, only actions of a certain kind are noted, fully and within their context. Breux (1974) for example, made observations of student 'protest crowds', noting the spatial disposition of leaders and chant initiators, and Baxter (1970) measured the distance between people in a side by side position as they watched animals in a zoo, demonstrating that different intervals are adopted by different cultural groups.

The method may also be used in conjuction with a time interval, as when the number of events per given period is the measure required to compare one environment with another.

Naturalistic and controlled observation
A broad distinction is usefully drawn between naturalistic and controlled observation. In the former, behaviour is observed in a natural setting with minimum intrusion by the observer. In the latter, the situation is stage managed to make observation easier, hopefully with gains that outweigh the increased artificiality. For example, subjects might be asked to mark on a diagram how they would expect to arrange themselves at a table for certain activities involving, say, cooperation, competition or coaction (working on the same task but independently). Using naturalistic observation, it would be necessary

to follow the subjects until they sat at a table or to observe a limited number of tables where seating behaviour could be expected to take place. The economy of controlling the situation (and its corresponding dangers) are obvious.

All forms of questionnaire and interview are, in this sense, controlled observation. So also is the use of simulation in presenting models or photographs to represent the environmental stimuli. Kuethe (1962), for example, has developed a method for studying social *schemata* (i.e. normative perceptions about how objects and people arrange themselves in space) by asking subjects to arrange cutout figures on a board. It will also be evident that there is no sharp boundary between controlled observation and experimentation, for control is the essence of the latter. Once the observer asks himself 'how would he respond if I . . .?' he is almost over the brink.

The experiment

The aim of an experiment is always to test one or more specific hypotheses. For observation, prior hypotheses may be desirable but by no means essential; findings may be borne from the data. A hypothesis is like an equation, a statement that two sets of events, e.g. crowding-aggression or isolation-territoriality are related to each other. These variables are named the independent and dependent variable because the former is deliberately manipulated and the changes dependent on it are then observed and measured. All that is meant by experimental manipulation is that the independent variable be changed through several 'levels' and this is usually done factorially, i.e. with two or more 'conditions' at predetermined levels (see A8). There is, however, no logical limit to the number of discrete steps in variables, and an experiment can be analysed using a correlation co-efficient between the independent and dependent variables as legitimately as by a test of the difference in means of the dependent variable for two conditions of the independent variable.

The major decision that has to be taken in designing any psychological experiment is whether to administer the various levels of the independent variable to the same subjects on successive occasions, or to quite separate groups of subjects. The differences are entirely ones of 'control'. In the former case, many potential sources of interference arising from the subjects' personalities or abilities will not arise, but 'order effects' are troublesome. The subjects are more practised or more fatigued, or just different, on a second observation and this confounds the outcome. If separate groups of subjects are used, there are no order effects but one begins with tiresome differences between the subjects in their likely response to the independent variables.

The real difficulty of experiments lies not in manipulation of the independent variable or in measuring the consequences for the dependent variable, but in the control of *interfering* variables. Unless all factors that could simultaneously change the dependent variable are brought under control, no valid evidence can be adduced for the hypothesis (see A1, A8).

Control can be exercised in several ways. The most obvious is by eliminating interfering factors from the situation altogether, but this is sometimes impossible. If the effect of interfering variables can be measured, it may be possible to eliminate their contribution to the dependent variable by statistical means. The most common method is to balance the effect of interfering variables equally between the conditions of the experiment, so that their contribution to variance is nullified. This is done by *counter-balancing* the conditions over time (i.e. in the sequence abba or baab) in a 'same subjects' design or by 'matching' the subjects or situations in a 'different subjects' design.

It only remains to add that modern statistical methods make it possible, in fact desirable, to conduct experiments with several independent variables simultaneously.

A compendium of measurement techniques

The dictionary definition of a compendium is a 'comprehensive and compact list'. By these exacting criteria the compendium of methods that is given as an appendix to this chapter is deficient on both counts. However, it is offered as a first approximation in the hope that it will evolve by refinement and extension.

The justification for the attempt is the need for researchers and appraisers to have a check list of methods which they can scan before making a decision about the best tools for use in a particular job. Such a list can trigger new ideas that may not immediately occur to the inexperienced (the range of possibilities is too wide for even the experienced to be able to dispense with a systematic review), and may also serve as a reminder of the virtues and shortcomings that characterize each class of methods. It may also alert intending researchers to what is being measured. Too many people choose first to 'do a survey' or to 'give a questionnaire' and hardly stop to consider whether they are attempting to observe behaviour, attitudes or perceptions or whether they have chosen the best available method.

A compendium of measurement methods

Type of Human Response	General Mode	Method
1. BEHAVIOUR	1.1 Directly recorded at time of behaviour	1. Behaviour mapping-observers using behaviour and position coding
		2. Observation of behaviour settings, verbal description
		3. Time lapse photography/video-sound recording
		4. Interception and monitoring of messages
		5. Hodometer (automatic floor contact recording)
		6. Path recording by tracking
		7. Behaviour check-lists used by observer
		8. Tracking by L.F. radio
		9. Samples of performance, i.e. 'psychological tests'
		10. Physiological recording during task performance, e.g. electromyography, cardiovascular response
		11. Recording of spatial position on floor grid-iron pattern by observers
		12. Activity self-reports by time sampling
		13. Counting and/or classifying of dyadic encounters

Type of Human Response	General Mode	Method
	1.2 Indirectly recorded from subjects	1. Observers using rating scales post hoc, summary
		2. Use of official documents, statistics, etc. which record behaviour
		3. Information tests
		4. Retrospective case studies
		5. Interest tests
		6. Follow-up of occupancy changes, houses or rooms
		7. Follow-up of physical modifications to building found necessary
		8. Analysis of 'complaints'/ 'suggestions'
		9. Analysis of wear and tear and other semi-permanent traces of activity, e.g. nose prints on display cases, footprints in mud or snow, etc.
		10. Content analysis of newspapers and other writing
		11. Use of models, dolls etc. to reproduce behaviour
	1.3 Verbal report by subject of past or current behaviour	1. Interviews
		2. Questionnaires
		3. Behaviour self report schedules
		4. Sociometric analysis of reported behaviour
		5. Poll and open-ended survey questions
2. FEELINGS AND EMOTIONS (including aesthetic pleasure)	2.1 Directly recorded	1. Physiological recording of autonomic nervous system activity; pupil dilation, psycho-galvanic response, electroencephalography, cardiovascular responses, etc.
	2.2 Indirectly recorded	1. By inference from behaviour; smiles, sighs, duration of voluntary pauses, yawns, variance in attention
		2. By inference from performance tasks designed to reflect mood,

Type of Human Response	General Mode	Method
		e.g. makes judgements of facial expressions
	2.3 Post hoc verbal report	As for attitudes, 4.2 and 4.3
3. ATTENTION PERCEPTIONS COGNITIONS	3.1 Post hoc representation: graphic	1. Cognitive maps or schemata boundaries 2. Route maps 3. Image maps, i.e. with detail 4. Lewinian 'life space' diagrams 5. Social schemata (Kuenthe) 6. Selective recall tasks 7. Image sampling on spatial basis, e.g. street names, room numbers, furniture positions 8. Psycho-physical measures of perceived distance, direction 9. Reproduction of body image 10. Choice of equivalent structure from range
	3.2 Post hoc representation: verbal	1. Adjective check lists 2. Semantic differential 3. Repertory grids 4. Scales, refined by factor analysis 5. Scales, cumulative (Guttman) 6. Psarchigraphs (Canter) 7. Free description of schemata 8. Q-sorts
4. ATTITUDES/ PREFERENCES	4.1 Non verbal projective	1. Binocular rivalry 2. Tachistoscopic presentation 3. Cartoon strips with empty 'balloons' (Rosenweig) 4. Ambiguous situations (Proshansky) 5. Use of models, dolls etc. to elicit attitudes, e.g. privacy
	4.2 Verbal, Unstructured	1. Open ended questionnaire 2. Interviews 3. Sentence completion 4. Story completion

Type of Human Response	General Mode	Method
	4.3 Verbal, Structured	1. Scales, custom built (e.g. Thurstone, Likert, Guttman etc.) or standardized
		2. Forced choice instruments
		3. Paired comparisons
		4. Ranking stimuli according to criteria, i.e. preferences
		5. Information tests
		6. Sociometry (matrices, indices and diagrammatic representations of friendship choice)

4
Houses and homes

The house is the most common of all buildings. Its purpose is to provide an environment for the family that will enable the members to meet their individual basic needs of eating, sleeping, washing, defecating, dressing, relaxing – and their multifarious social activities, discussing, entertaining, making love, rearing children. Even this short list suggests that the building, though small, has to be more flexible than almost any other.

It also provides for needs more fundamental to existence than most, so its inadequacies, when they occur, are more damaging. The development of the inner layers of personality is cradled in the house, the social structures of marriage and parenthood are nurtured there. It becomes, like our clothes, an extension of the self and of the family's personality.

Fortunately, it is an environment that we can select, shape and personalize more than any other. So much so, in fact, that there is a school of thought in architecture that says all we have to do is provide housing in great variety and with internal flexibility and all outstanding problems will solve themselves. The idea has panache, but this loses its shine when viewed from a position of less prosperity, less mobility, less social class, in fact, than is generally enjoyed by architects and psychologists. Variety of ground plan costs money, or could be achieved only at the expense of fewer houses. We are forced to compromise on that one. Flexibility, such as movable partitions, is also very costly either in money or in privacy, although there is some scope for technology and for 'open plan' imaginativeness. Mobility costs money; even a move to a house which is different in style and layout but judged equal in value. But perhaps most important of all, people do not normally live in houses but in 'residential settings'. The whole social–spatial schema of a familiar physical locality and its neighbours, friends and enemies is a context of profound importance. This applies particularly to the roles of housewife and mother which are frequently constrained within its limits.

Hence, although people are adaptable and what Rapaport (1969) has called 'loose fit' design is always desirable, there are severe limits to the variety of house form and layout that can be provided. This and the sheer number involved makes it extremely important that optimal designs are chosen.

It has been argued by a leading writer on architectural design that the arrangement of furniture provides the only scope for flexibility in a house and that this has nothing to do with the architect. We may agree with the former but not the latter. The work of the Building Research Establishment has shown that the size, shape and internal disposition of rooms is of great importance to the occupiers. Furthermore, there are many features of the building which limit the arrangements that can be made with the furniture. The positions and width of doors and whether they slide or hinge, the height and shape of windows, the presence of hatches and so on all have their effects. Also, the furniture and fittings in the bathroom and kitchen are integral to the house and need to be specified if not designed directly by the architect.

Specialist rooms

It has been estimated that the housewife spends an average of four hours per day working in the kitchen and compatability between her anatomical dimensions and the design of the furniture and fittings can conserve substantial quantities of energy. A study by Saville (1970) used the methods of ergonomics. For example, the contractions of the main muscle groups in the legs and backs of a sample of women were measured (by attached electrodes) while they worked; markers were fixed to the bony landmarks, i.e. the shoulder, elbow, wrist, hip and ankle, and photographed in movement to give accurate observations of posture; subjects were placed on a stability platform

66

in order to measure the relative weight displacements which impose muscular efforts in maintaining equilibrium.

The current British Standard for sink heights was found to be suitable only for a group of *short* housewives, and one important recommendation that emerged was the need for two work surface heights, with food preparation lower than sink height. In the not too distant future we may judge it primitive to be aiming at compatability by adopting the mean as optimal. This is merely the single figure that suits the largest number (assuming a symetrical frequency distribution) and we would require several alternative dimensions to achieve compatability with a large number – as we do already with garment sizes. The objections on grounds of economy would be largely removed if plumbing connections were made flexible, so that height could be adjusted with blocks or screw feet.

Studies from the Building Research Establishment have pointed to the very wide range of activities the kitchen is required to accommodate. They include family conferences, group therapy, filling in the pools coupon and repairing bicycles. There is strong resistance to house designs which imply that working people should eat meals in a compartment separate from the kitchen. They would prefer to stand up for breakfast in the kitchen than relax expansively in a 'dinette'.

The bathroom, according to exhaustive work by Kira (1957) could also be designed to increase its compatability with human needs, physiology and particularly attitudes to privacy. The data for the study were derived from a field survey of a thousand households and from a laboratory investigation in which a small group of subjects were filmed while carrying out personal hygiene and elimination routines under experimentally varied conditions.

One of the unexpected findings from the field survey was that the bathroom was used as a privacy sanctuary for an extraordinary range of activities beyond its primary ones. One might suggest a need for a small alcove for books and magazines, for example, among the ceramics and chrome. Also, the provision normally made by architects for the storage of medicines and cosmetics and other domestic objects not intended for the use of children is normally quite inadequate.

The very strong need to be visually private is matched by the desire not to be heard, or for ones whereabouts not to be

67

sensed in any other way, and this has implications for the location of the room, its entrance, its size, location, window glazing and for its acoustical treatment.

Similar ergonomic studies have been made of the bedroom and of sleeping behaviour and the latter might be taken as a timely reminder of the interactive relationship between behaviour and environment. Careful anthropometric studies and time lapse photographic records might lead one to suppose that sleeping postures and movements demand larger beds. But anyone with a moderate range of experience will know that there is a well established postulate of human sleeping behaviour, namely, that people expand to fill the bed space available. Hence, the bed determines posture as well as posture determining the choice of bed.

The meaning of furniture

In discussing kitchens and bathrooms our emphasis has been on achieving compatability with the behavioural characteristics of the occupants. But furniture arrangements also involve an attempt to achieve aesthetic pleasure in the home and convey meaning. Although these can only be separated with difficulty from functional utility, one would expect some degree of consistency to emerge in taste and arrangement according, for example, to social class or age; also that the architect should be aware of such trends so that he can either cater to them or, if he feels justified in attempting to improve them, he can at least know where he is starting from.

For Local Authority housing there is some evidence of the degree to which this knowledge is attained. In a Cardiff study (Edwards, 1974) a comparison was made between furniture items and their arrangement as actually observed in the living room of 232 houses with identical ground plans and the expectations of twenty-eight architects who were normally involved in the design of similar houses. Cluster analysis of the data confirmed that there is quite a high degree of consistency in tenants' arrangements, but there were very few architects whose expectations corresponded. Only half of them, for example, predicted the most popular position for the television set. Only 7 per cent of armchair placements were allocated by the architects to the wall positions immediately adjacent to the hearth on each side, but that is where 50 per cent of tenants had placed them. Fig. 4.1 shows the actual and predicted arrangements for dining tables, where again, there is a large disparity.

Tenants' dining tables

0	5	0	1	1
13	0	0	0	14
8	4	3	2	23

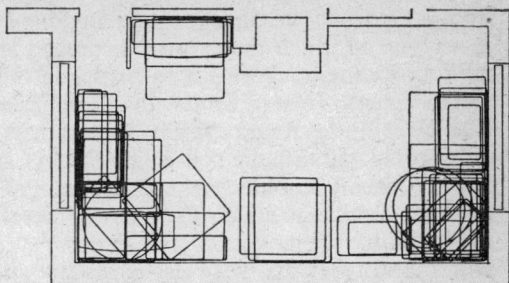

Architects' dining tables

0	0	0	0	0
5	0	0	0	5
2	2	0	0	1

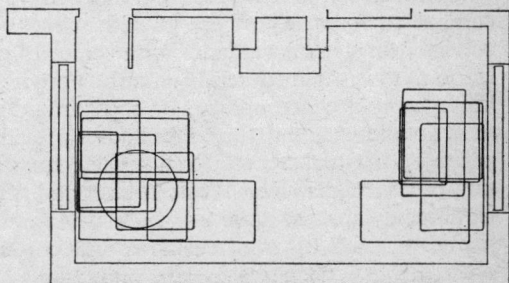

Fig. 4.1 *From Edwards (1974)*

Some of the most revealing evidence from this study emerges from the tape recorded remarks by the architects. They valued clear circulation space and also tended to divide the room into 'activity zones'. The tenants, on the other hand, seemed to be much more concerned with creating a 'pleasing display'.

Although a house is a flexible space, this kind of mis-match between the designer and the consumer seems excessive and there would seem to be a strong case for much closer observation of the ways in which people actually use their spaces and furniture.

Another process that may be reflected in choice and arrangement of furnishings, as with clothes, is what Goffman (1963) has called 'impression management'. There is little direct causal evidence for this because it is difficult to disentangle people's conformity to the groups of which they are members from their deliberate choice of the signalling systems belonging to a group to which they aspire. Laumann and House (1970) used an extensive check list to catalogue the items in nearly 1,000 homes. It was found that established 'upper class' WASPs (White Anglo Saxon Protestants) had traditional tastes compared with the non-Anglo Saxon Catholic 'Moderns', but the socially ambitious among the latter showed a tendency to adopt traditional styles. Even more interesting, consistency in furnishings (regardless of style or decor) was associated with political attitudes that were also consistent and relatively more extreme.

A similar picture emerges from the study of a set of Japanese company houses. These are graded in size and appear to be allocated in strict accordance with seniority within the organization. This seniority tends to correlate with the stage in the life cycle and hence number of occupants, but in such a way that, notwithstanding, the larger houses provide more space per person. This makes possible a greater functional differentiation of the rooms along Western lines and departing from the traditional Japanese style in which a few ubiquitous items of furniture, such as mats, cushions and coat-stand are moved according to changing needs and time of the day into a few multi-purpose spaces controlled by the fusuma (sliding screen).

Hence, in this case we have a similar process operating in the opposite direction from Laumann and House's study. In Japan, Westernization (which includes the acquisition of television sets, dining suites and refrigerators) is only possible with a large house and this means that social class is positively correlated with modernism and not with traditionalism. One of the fascinating questions that this raises is how far the differentiation of room function leads (through changes in activities) to a different, more autonomous social structure like our own, and how far cultural changes induce changes in social structure which in turn demand spatial differentiation. It is likely that both processes are operating.

There is little doubt that the way in which furniture is arranged in a room or house conveys 'meaning' or implications of how to behave for someone who enters. These may be mediated either through the feelings or moods that the stimuli provoke or the 'behaviour plans' that are suggested by the physical objects and their arrangement. Often these effects operate below the threshold of consciousness and, indeed, the 'presenter' must in some situations be wary of displaying such environmental inducers too obviously, lest he be suspected of attempting to manipulate behaviour. This may be transparent in extreme cases. The intending seducer does not therefore place the couch in the centre of the room but unobtrusively in a corner – with perhaps a deep pile rug in front of the fire as a transitional signal. We shall return to the use of these deliberate or unconsciousness signalling tactics in a later section after considering the possibilities inherent in rooms for inducing particular feelings or moods.

Affective responses to rooms

One of the earliest controlled experiments in environmental psychology was a comparison of the effects of 'a beautiful', 'an average' and 'an ugly' room. The former was a comfortable study, furnished with elegance and taste and the latter was a cleaner's store containing buckets, brooms and a garbage can. Strictly speaking they were not domestic rooms, but it is probably safe to generalize the results.

The subtle feature of the experiment was that the subjects were not required to carry out a performance task, such as the cancellation of letters or the addition of digits so much favoured by early psychologists, but a judgemental task. They were required to assess some ambiguous photographs of faces on rating scales from 'energetic' to 'fatigued' and from 'well-being' to 'displeasure'. It was hypothesized that the subjects' own moods would be reflected in these judgements and that they would differ according to the environment. This was confirmed, but a further sagacious twist in the design was to use graduate students to administer the tests and to rotate them through the various conditions in the laudable interests of 'counter balancing' and to ask them to complete the rating scales to familiarize themselves with the procedure and, at the end of sessions, to 'check for reliability'. This non-reactive condition yielded not only a confirmation of the main effect

71

but also some additional evidence at the behavioural level by showing that the 'experimenters' lingered longer over the testing in the beautiful room and made short shrift of the ugly ones (Mintz, 1956).

The independent variable in this experiment was simply a package of qualities in each case which by common consent added up to beauty and ugliness respectively. A systematic series of experiments on room impression conducted by Wools and Canter (1970) adopted a more analytical approach, attempting to explain some of the components. Their independent variables were ceiling angle (sloping or horizontal), window shape and seating arrangement. These were manipulated through a series of line drawings of room interiors. Some examples are shown in Fig. 4.2.

The dependent variable was 'friendliness', one of several dimensions (the others were 'activity' and 'harmony') identified as important in the perception of rooms by factor analysis of a much larger number of semantic differential scales. In effect, the friendliness measuring instrument includes a selection of those polar opposite scales which had previously been found to run in the same direction, such as welcoming–unwelcoming; soft–hard; and, of course, friendly–unfriendly. The selection of these is not arbitrary – but based on intercorrelations. The naming of the combination is a matter for the experimenters judgement. He selects the label (not necessarily employed in the sub-scales) which best summarizes the pervasive character of the constituent scales.

Osgood's original work on the semantic differential identified three major components underlying his scales. These were evaluation (good–bad; useful–useless), potency (strong–weak; sharp–blunt) and activity (moving–still; active–passive) and these have recurred in many subsequent studies. However, these, like Osgood's, have been studies mainly concerned with the whole range of meaning in language – the dimensions underlying more limited areas of experience such as buildings are bound to be different. In this context, there has been good agreement between an increasing number of studies that buildings are responded to on dimensions of 'friendliness', 'harmony', 'tidiness', and 'comfort'. These are probably subdivisions of Osgood's 'evaluation' and Wools also identified a dimension similar to Osgood's 'activity'.

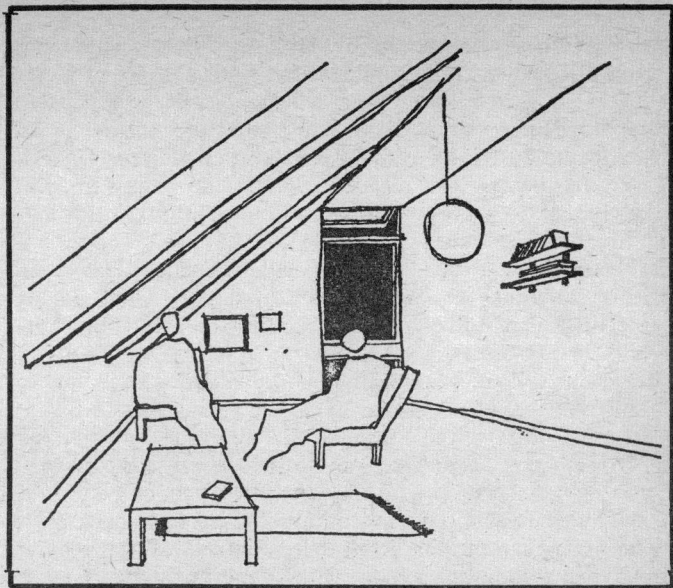

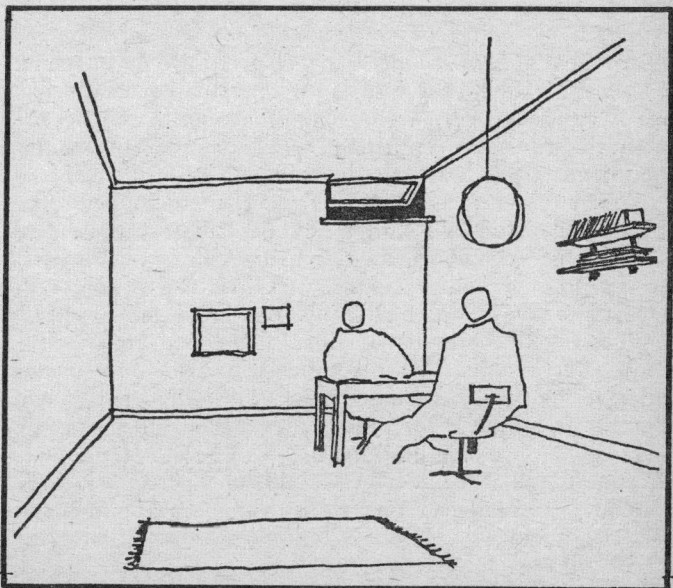

Fig. 4.2 *The 'most friendly' and 'least friendly' rooms*
(Wools and Canter, 1970)

In parentheses it should be remarked that one cannot catch a dimension in the sophisticated statistical net of factor analysis unless the relevant polar adjectival scales are included in the trawl. For example, *warmth* cannot emerge as one of the critical underlying factors in people's perceptions of buildings unless the original questionnaires include items such as tepid–cold, ardent–cool, sunny–dull, balmy–wintry, fervent–dull. More recent studies along these lines have followed the admirable example of Kelly's Personal Construct Theory in eliciting the adjectives ('constructs') that are actually used by people instead of relying on the experimenter to supply the likely ones.

To return to Wools and Canter's findings, they were able to demonstrate that the room designed with a sloping ceiling is consistently perceived as more friendly than the conventional one. It is interesting to speculate on the reasons for this, perhaps it is an association with the romantic garret or perhaps it is a bucolic connection with farm buildings or barn dances.

The other main finding from these studies was that seating arrangements endowed a room with friendliness and this has a more obvious explanation in their implications of social interaction.

It can be argued that judgements of line drawings of rooms are so artificial that they cannot be generalized to real situations. There is, however, accumulating evidence that the meaning attaching to these simulations, which enormously ease the experimenter's task, is not substantially different from real life. Within the present context, Wools and Canter supplied some confirmation of this by testing both the reliability and validity of their experimental set-up. Using housewives as subjects, they first showed that if the scales were used to give comparative assessments of two real rooms, one an elegant one and the other a store room, they distinguished effectively and also gave reliable measures, i.e. the scores coincided for two successive testings of the same subject. They then gave their subjects a task, that is the rating of a set of line drawings of rooms for 'harmony' in both the beautiful and the ugly room and found the expected interaction, i.e. people perceive a drawing as more harmonious if they are assessing it in a harmonious or friendly room.

The role of the open fire as a focal point for social interaction in rooms must go back into pre-history and, certainly, it is within living memory for most people that its warmth has been essential to comfort. Increasingly, however, it is no more than a symbol – but one whose continuing potency is well known to the proselytizer of gas fires and 'magic coal' radiant electric fires. Are they well advised in attempting to exploit these associations? Do we still derive pleasure and are we still influenced to behave in particular ways by the glow and flicker of the hearth – or is the television perhaps taking over this critical role?

In a factorial experiment, subjects were presented with a series of photographs showing rooms with and without a fire and a television and with seating focused either inwards or outwards towards the focal object and either closely or widely spaced. They were asked to assess the suitability of each arrangement for 'chatting', 'having a party', 'reading' and 'doing physical exercises'. One clear result was that the more passive activities of reading and chatting were judged significantly more compatible not only with the 'fire only' condition but also with the two chair arrangement oriented towards the focus and not facing towards each other. This is redolent of Sommer's finding that 'along side' positions at a table are judged more suitable for co-orientation or cooperation while opposite facing implies competition.

The design and layout of the whole house and garden have obvious similar implications for social behaviour, but we know very little about the range and power of these. The largest changes in the demands made on a house depend on stages in the life cycle of the family and not infrequently people make the somewhat procrustean attempt to fit their changing way of life into the same house rather than cope with the upheaval of moving to another.

Quantity of space is perhaps more crucial than its arrangement and the transitory nature of this can be nicely illustrated from a survey of garden needs carried out by the Building Research Establishment.

Gradual changes have been taking place over the years in people's attitudes towards gardens and the use to which they should be put. These are not easy to discern because of the periodic influence of national food crises which produce many temporary gardeners. There are also large regional differences, with only 58 per cent of houses in the north-west having gardens compared with 80 per cent in the rest of Britain.

Overall, garden space is judged increasingly to be desirable as a place for children to play and for simply 'sitting out', but car ownership, particularly among those with small gardens (under 800 square feet), reduces interest in gardening with 48 per cent instead of 64 per cent regarding it as a principal way in which space should be used. The increasing tendency for housewives to have jobs outside the home is also having its effects, with 27 per cent of working wives judging the garden to be too small compared with 33 per cent of non-working wives.

These figures are derived from a survey of households in Harlow and Basildon new towns and in Sheffield (Cook, 1969). But the most striking evidence provided by this survey is the important but transitory nature of the demand for garden space for children's play. Since older children much prefer to play outside the home (and once safety considerations have been taken care of, this would seem to be essential for the necessary scope and complexity of both physical and social environment), the period during which the garden is needed for play is very short despite the contrary impression that may sometimes be formed by parents: '... assuming a two year spacing of births in a family complete with three children, all three will be of an age to make maximum use of the garden for only three or four years.'

The data shown in Fig. 4.3 nicely demonstrates a relationship between garden-size, family-size and satisfaction. With a garden of 900 square feet, all but about 25 per cent of families with three children find the space adequate, but below this the number of children is critical. An inverse relationship between number of children and interest in gardens is shown in Fig. 4.3 (2) and this is to be expected, but it is gratifying to

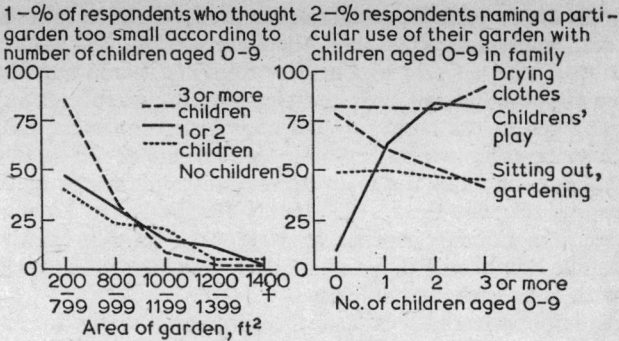

1 – % of respondents who thought garden too small according to number of children aged 0–9.

2 – % respondents naming a particular use of their garden with children aged 0–9 in family

3 or more children
1 or 2 children
No children

Drying clothes
Childrens' play
Sitting out, gardening

Area of garden, ft²

No. of children aged 0–9

Fig. 4.3 *From Cook (1969)*

see that 'sitting out' is not affected. Again, this may run counter to the perceptions of parents.

Territoriality in the home

Territoriality, the acquisition of an area of space and set of physical objects for personal occupation, undoubtedly occurs even in those parts of the home that are supposedly 'public'. Although we lack evidence on this for family situations it can be safely inferred from the observations made in old people's homes (where the defence of space is particularly determined) and from experimental isolation studies of servicemen and field observations of arctic explorers.

The social importance of territorial behaviour in the home is probably best understood by referring to several functional advantages that it yields, rather than invoking the more esoteric 'instinctive need' type explanation, based on dubious analogies with animal behaviour.

Territoriality endows privacy and ensures a relative freedom from interference with one's activities. Space is a commodity which is essential to every activity and for the space to be unencumbered is sometimes essential, and normally desirable. Even more important, the various spaces in a house, as in any other building, are a reflection of the social organization which they are designed to contain.

77

People are performing social roles in the family such as cook, gardener, handyman, accountant, chauffeur, student, dishwasher and nurse. The ways in which these roles are shared out, the degree of specialization and their changing importance at different stages in the family's history all dictate different uses of the space. The availability of space determines the degree of overlap of functions and it is within most people's experience to observe that the same *basic* family functions can be performed in a holiday caravan as were performed in family homes like Blenheim Palace or Longleat, which resemble small towns in their spatial complexity.

The important thing is that the space should fit the integrated pattern of roles – it should be isomorphic with this pattern. Such compatibility may be helped by the designer but it also depends a great deal on the social norms and rules, explicit or implicit, which are devised by a family to regulate the usage of scarce space. These may include priority allocations – e.g. 'father sits there' (often a focal position near the hearth from which all other seating positions may be directly observed) if he is at home, but otherwise the space *may* be occupied by others; also there are temporal rules, such as certain spaces can be used for homework or sewing when not in demand for eating. The degree of social harmony is a function, then, both of the design space and of the social processes. The Japanese people are a notable example of the ways in which very small allocations of space can none the less be occupied harmoniously if everyone knows and scrupulously follows the social–spatial rules.

There is, of course, an obverse to these precepts. When organizations become large, the rules about the uses of space cannot be learned by the members of the group unless they are relatively simple. Rooms are endowed with 'labels' and this severely limits multiple and flexible usage. The same thing may happen in a home where a particular function is judged by the powerful members of the group (usually the parents!) to be of superordinate importance so that the 'front parlour' for example is maintained as a 'persona space' to impress occasional visitors in spite of severe pressure on space elsewhere in the house.

It is remarkable, of course, that despite the huge proportion of our gross national product which is spent on home building, we have almost no systematic evidence of how families use houses. It is safe to say that we don't even know how we use our own house and might be very surprised by such data. It may be argued by architects that house space has 'evolved' by successive adjustments until the shoe doesn't pinch. On the other hand, there is plenty of evidence from other fields that adjustments do not happen in this way, or happen only very slowly in the absence of effective feedback. People may adjust to a poorly fitting shoe at the expense of freedom of activity and perhaps in the long term, by developing a distorted gait.

One admirable effort to study home behaviour has been made by Smith *et al* (1969). A complete three bedroom dwelling was constructed and a total of 20 five-person families were observed in great detail as they lived in it for two weeks. One reaction is to regard this as a most ambitious project but, of course, it is trivial in scope in the face of the potential gains from such research. The authors were the first to recognize that the investigation has severe limitations, not only in sample size and duration but also in the artificiality of the almost 'holidaylike' situation, and in the fact that the occupants were volunteers and they were being observed by people stationed throughout the home scoring interaction check lists and similar instruments.

However, such studies are a beginning, and although some of the results are obvious, this cannot be said of them all. For example, women with families at *all* stages of the life cycle, from Type I with pre-school children to Type IV with a retired husband and adult children, spent about the same amount of time during daylight in the house – and it was surely high at 80 to 84 per cent. Also, husbands with pre-school or school age children spent only 36 and 37 per cent respectively of their time in the house whereas those with adult children spent 53 per cent. They were all professional or business families and it seems that the husbands removed themselves during the evenings to pursue their work or other interests with a greater chance of privacy.

5
School buildings and pupil behaviour

It has already been emphasized that the design of buildings may have its most potent influence on behaviour indirectly, i.e. by facilitating or promoting particular forms of social organization. This is nowhere more evident than in educational buildings.

Social influences on learning

In 1897 Triplett conducted what was probably the first formal laboratory experiment in the social aspects of education. He had noticed, from official records of the bicycle races much in vogue at that time, that the performance of *individuals* speeded up by no less than 20 per cent in the presence of another 'pacing' bicycle. He set up his laboratory experiment to compare the performance of children working alone and in company. The task was the winding of fishing reels and *group* performance was found to be appreciably better.

Allport (1920) later invented the term 'social facilitation' to describe the increment in performance that was found in situations where people are engaged individually on the same task in each other's presence but without any apparent communication. In many subsequent experiments the effect was found to be more limited than had been thought and its explanation more complex. The increment was shown only for relatively simple, repetitive tasks and, indeed, there was sometimes a fall-off in performance of tasks calling for intellectual concentration. It was also found that the co-workers need not be physically present in the same room; it is enough that they be perceived by the subject to be engaged on the same task, somewhere.

· Interest in the process went into abeyance, but there has been a revival in recent years with the application of the concept of *arousal* and the Yerkes–Dodson law, which asserts that there is an optimum level of physiological activation or 'arousal' for every task. The presence of other people is clearly arousing, at any rate in the early stages. This may be an instinctive response originating from defence or mating situations which has survived because of its obvious functional value. But it is certainly also a learned posture of implicit or explicit competitiveness within our kind of society. Other work in psychology has shown that the presence of an 'audience' person has similarly enhancing or disruptive effects.

Audience studies. Bergum and Lehr (1963) used a simple 'vigilance' task in which young servicemen had to monitor a display to detect occasional errors in a pattern of lights. In one condition they worked for two hours fifteen minutes in isolation and in another they were told that a senior officer would drop in now and then to check. The former showed the usual progressive deterioration in performance; the latter remained stable.

But in experiments involving the learning of nonsense syllables, the solving of block puzzles and performance on a pursuit rotor, for example, the audience had an overall disruptive effect. Wapner and Alper (1952) measured decision time to select one of two words which best fitted the sense of a given phrase and compared performance with a single-person audience, consisting of one staff member; an unseen audience of one staff and three students; and the same audience while it was visible in the room. The first of these conditions was the best.

In both social facilitation and audience effects, spatial factors are obviously important, but they have rarely been directly manipulated as independent variables. An exception is the well known situation contrived by Milgram (1965) to measure 'obedience' (see B1). This has some components of audience and also of social conformity pressure, another process that is heavily involved in situations of learning and instruction, not simply for imposing sanctions but for setting example. Milgram found that a disturbingly high proportion of subjects could be induced to obey the instructions of a high status person to deliver what seemed to be extremely dangerous electric shocks to a person in the adjacent room in spite of the fact that groans of protest and sounds of pain were being emitted from the victim. It should be mentioned that the 'victim' was a 'confederate' of the experimenter. In one experiment, Milgram varied the physical distance of the experimenter from the person imposing the shocks and found that the strength of obedience pressure increased inversely with distance.

An explanation in terms of the intrusion of 'personal space' could be advanced here, but the concept tends to be merely descriptive rather than explanatory unless we are prepared to argue that the size of human personal space is determined instinctively and therefore has some critical range (see Ch. 2). It would seem more parsimonious to say that we learn, in childhood and onwards, that other persons can carry out repertoires of behaviour (to our advantage or disadvantage) that vary as a function of their *proximity*. Distance also influences the visibility of the other person and hence the communication of his intentions, but environmental factors influence the extent to which attitudes can be communicated.

Incidentally, a so far untested prediction from this would be that children are more susceptible than adults to arousal from proximity, because such a high proportion of their outcomes such as smacks, sweets and pats on the head are mediated by close contact.

Perceived standards of performance

To the extent that there is implicit competition in the social facilitation and audience paradigms, it must be assumed that the subject forms at least a notional estimate of the opposition, i.e. the standard of performance desired or expected. Even when this becomes completely internalized so that the subject is competing with himself, i.e. with 'self respect' at stake, it can be argued that he is operating to a social norm.

A demonstration that the effects of standard setting can be

distinguished from arousal is provided by an experiment by Foot and Lee (1970).

Three subjects simultaneously performed a simple score-able learning task in adjacent booths. Display panels in each booth could show the subjects their own score and that of their two colleagues. This 'group learning' was found to be far superior to solitary learning. The next problem was to discover *why* – and this was attempted by separating two important aspects of the task. In one condition (audience; no feedback) the subject could not see the display panels of his two co-workers – but thought they could see his. In the other condition (feedback; no audience) the subject could monitor the scores of his co-workers but thought that he was himself performing in complete privacy. The results are shown in Fig. 5.1.

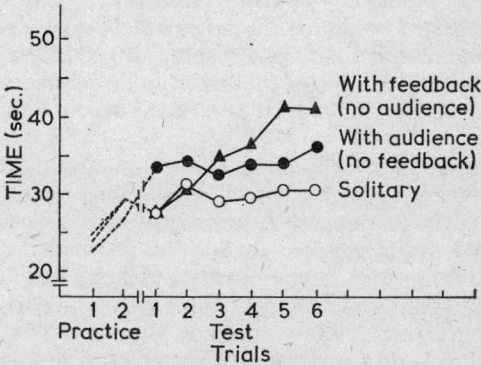

Fig. 5.1 *Mean trial scores for three performance conditions (Foot and Lee, 1970)*

It will be seen that 'audience arousal' yields an increment even before the scores of others are seen – but this advantage remains fairly stable. The norm receiving condition, however, gives a much steeper and progressive learning curve than the solitary one, indicating that subjects attempt to emulate or excel a social norm.

Communication of 'content' information. In the majority of social learning situations, however, much more is intercommunicated than a stimulus to arousal and a rough standard of

83

performance. If members of a group are each attempting to perform the same task, but in parellel (the conventional school situation), a good deal of information about the changing standards of others is available as feedback but there is also information about different ways of performing the task and their relative pay-offs. The teacher is the obvious but by no means the only source of the latter communications.

Perlmutter and Montmollin (1952) used a form of 'public acclamation' for the group learning of a list of nonsense syllables. On each attempt one member or another could deliver the correct syllables until the whole list could be run through more or less in unison. The average individual learning achieved was greater by this method than by the control group arrangement in which each person learned by himself. Similar results were obtained by Gurnee (1962) with a bolthead maze, a series of paired boltheads the selection of one of which was 'correct' and would light up a display. He found, moreover, that subjects on the edge of the crowd followed the more confident central ones but nonetheless learned better than when alone.

As examples of the (attempted) intercommunication of the same responses by each subject, these two experiments represent a social learning situation that now occurs somewhat infrequently within our formal educational system. In the past it was used for rote learning of poetry and multiplication tables. In work situations it occurs more commonly, as a part of problem solving activities of a more complex kind. That is, the capacity of a group to carry a larger store of memory than any single member is one of the factors than may endow it with superiority.

However, the situation in which these advantages are maximized, is one where the memory store or skills held by each of the individuals is *complementary*. The members are not attempting, with varying success, to remember the same thing but deliberately concentrating on contributing something different but essential to the solution (see B2).

The role of spatial factors in this kind of problem solving were simulated and shown to be important in the classic work of Leavitt (1951). Five-person teams were seated at a round table and separated, not by physical distance, but by functional distance. This was done by the ingenious device of dividing them with screens and allowing only limited communication through a system of hatchways via which written messages could be passed. The resulting communication networks, characterized as the 'circle', 'chain', 'wheel' and 'Y' had different levels of problem solving efficiency, and later research showed that they had implications also for leadership and popularity attributions. For example, if a person is placed spatially in a position of centrality in a communication network, he is likely to emerge as a leader whatever his personal qualities might be.

In situations where getting the right answer is the main object of the exercise, groups may be judged superior to individuals if they reach a solution more rapidly and more accurately than what are called 'nominal' groups (i.e. the same number of members chosen at random and working separately but given credit if one member succeeds in solving the problem). However, as already mentioned, the latter yields little educational profit for the unsuccessful members except for 'failure feedback' which is a spur of somewhat uncertain effectiveness (see C4).

The types of task which favour group superiority are those where the problem has multiple parts and the members have different capabilities. To gain optimal advantage from group work requires rapid intercommunication. This may mean a completely open structure or one organized in a conducive way, e.g. by the appointment of a leader or teacher, and with rules about who should contribute what and when to some form of agenda.

The communication of information about the task itself assumes much greater importance in this kind of situation than in parallel group learning, but although people are all doing their different thing they also have implicit norms by which to measure who is doing a good job and who is not – so some elements of competition still obtain. Also, conditions may be arranged so that there is more than one group and a communication system that facilitates competition *between* them (see B2). Again, the size and spatial arrangement of the building container may render possible a social structure of this kind.

One would expect the design of schools and classrooms to be based on an analysis of the optimal ways of performing tasks of increasing difficulty, i.e. becoming more and more oriented to the kind of co-operative group problem solving that characterizes contemporary real life in work organizations. Instead, the developmental trend often seems to go the other way, with the oldest and cleverest pupils engaged in intensive solitary study or sitting in neat rows facing their instructor. There has been a burgeoning in project work, but paradoxically this has been concentrated more in the early, primary years and this may partially account for the disaffection of older pupils. At the spatial level, this is represented by a dramatic change in the furnishing and layout of primary schools that is not paralleled in secondary schools except where intrepid innovators have been at work (see C4).

However, the variety of social structures for different stages and kinds of learning activity is legion and it is only when we achieve a deeper understanding of them that we shall be able to design conducive environments. All we can do here is to indicate the potency of spatial factors by referring to studies of the classroom and wider settings.

The classroom setting

Space, play equipment and behaviour in nursery schools

Up to now, most of the studies in this tradition have been concerned to compare the effectiveness of different kinds of teacher style and little has been done on their physical setting. An exception is the work at Sheffield of Smith (1974) who, in an experimental playgroup, has been particularly concerned with the effects on children's behaviour of two variables – the amount of space and the amount of play equipment provided.

Work by some earlier investigators had tended to suggest, redolent of the studies of animal crowding, that children would be more aggressive in confined spaces. However, Connolly and Smith did not observe aggression as a function of space *per se* in their groups. The wider spaces did promote (or allow) a greater quantity of motor activity such as running, jumping and skipping, whereas these behaviours, as well as being less common in the confined space, took a different *form* with more recourse to the climbing frames and slides. The *quantity* of play equipment had a more marked influence. While surprisingly not lowering the quantity of 'fine handling movements' in play, the impoverished toy condition induced substantial changes in *social* organization. The average size of groups increased and more sharing occurred, although this was more in the nature of alternating or parallel uses of the equipment and could hardly be described as co-operative. Indeed, in this case, aggression and other forms of stress behaviour such as thumb-sucking tended to increase.

A later study suggests that co-operative behaviour might be induced by changing the *type* of physical play equipment as distinct from its quantity. This experiment compared play sessions with large objects e.g. a Wendy house, toy box and lid, stools, climbing frames etc. with similar sessions where jigsaws, teasets, blocks, a telephone and other small objects were made available. The former produced more talking, more physical contacts, more gross motor activity and more co-operation. The fantasy content of the interactions between the children, though less easy to evaluate, also appeared to be higher in the 'large toy' sessions, with the children engaging in such activities as sitting on a line of chairs as a pretend train, lining up chairs in the Wendy house to dance in front as a pretend theatre, etc.

Almost no research has been conducted on the degree of room partitioning that is possible in nursery school settings, despite the obvious importance of this question. An exception is an investigation which demonstrated that pre-school children do not seek the privacy of separate small activity rooms when these are offered, but appear to prefer a more social context. This is a preference they may retain until they are students (see below) although they are likely to discover that the specifically 'thinking' demands made on them even before age ten will be met more effectively, if less enjoyably in a distraction-free environment. Another study of partitioning looked at the social behaviour induced by a trefoil shaped playroom and found greater territory–defending behaviour and more aggression. The subjects in this case were mentally abnormal children and it would not be safe to generalize beyond this kind of hospital playroom application. However, it is in such situations that environmental design is particularly critical – providing a welcome increment of control where social forms of control are so limited.

'Open plan' classrooms and play spaces

The strong trend of English primary and nursery education is towards an open, creative, child-centred approach and away from the traditional fixed desk, 'look this way and pay attention' methods that grew from the Victorian Board schools (see C5). The old approach probably evolved less from educational principle than from expediency; a necessity to house large numbers of pupils so that the scarce resources of the teacher's direct verbal and visual communication could be administered to the largest numbers in the most economical space. The sheer tedium and impersonal nature of the process was doubtless responsible for creating a reluctance in the pupils, and the subsequent need for total surveillance, so that the teacher became raised on a podium at one end of a room with children facing her in rows in immutably fixed positions.

However, under the influence of Dewey, Montessori and Froebel who have advocated a more 'person centred' form of education, and of the 'progressives', such as Susan Isaacs and A. S. Neill, who have urged a much more liberal and democratic social organization within schools – there has been a gradual change over the past fifty years though it has been much less marked in secondary than in primary schools. The availability of cheap paper and pencils and all the more elaborate paraphernalia of classroom tools and equipment should not be under-estimated. Nor should the contribution of psychology in showing that there are large and measurable differences between individuals. Altogether, the trend has been towards a much more individualized, problem-centred and socially liberal form of education.

The environmental isomorph of this movement is the so-called 'open plan' school – in which the settings for different activities are dispersed into specialized bays and inlets with semi-partitions so that both children and teachers can move freely and easily from one setting to another (see Fig. 5.2).

The principal changes, for better or worse, are paradoxically more privacy – because the child is not chained cheek by jowl in a static space but able to perambulate freely. Secondly, hopefully, there is a more personal form of communication with teachers who are able to direct themselves to individual children or small groups rather than to the aggregate.

A study by Durlak and Lehman (1974) is part of a continu-

Fig. 5.2 From
Children and
their Primary
Schools (the
Plowden
Report),
Vol. I
(HMSO, 1967)

School for 320 Pupils Aged 3½ to 9 Years
Eveline Lowe School. Rolls Road, London, S.E. 1

This school was designed by the Department's Development Group in collaboration with the Inner London Education Authority within the current cost limit. The accommodation was planned for the following groupings of the 320 pupils:

Two "nursery" groups of 30 children (A and C on plan)
Four "family" groups of 40 children, with an age range of about two years (B, D, E, & F).
Two groups of older children, one of 40 (G) and one of 60 (H).
The last group was, of course, to be looked after by more than one teacher.
The main features to emerge, in the interpretation of the educational requirements in terms of planning for each of these eight groups were:

(a) The need to sub-divide the available space to allow a number of small groups of individuals to pursue widely varying activities.

(b) The need to make a distinction in character (i.e. in finishes, scale, colour, lighting, furniture) between a small, quiet carpeted area ; a general working area ; and an area equipped for messier kinds of work.

(c) The importance of direct access to a sheltered verandah and to the ground outside.

(d) The need to take into account the use of sizes of furniture from an early stage in design process.

There is no hard and last division between these group spaces and the rest of the school, for the whole environment (both inside and out) was conceived as potential 'teaching space', as opposed to a series of closed classrooms and 'non-teaching' areas. For example the arrangements for dining include a series of bays, furnished with tables and window seats, which look across to alternating display alcoves and window seats—an area designed not only for dining but as a small exhibition gallery and as working space for groups of individuals at other times of the day. The hall is equipped for a variety of large movement and drama work.

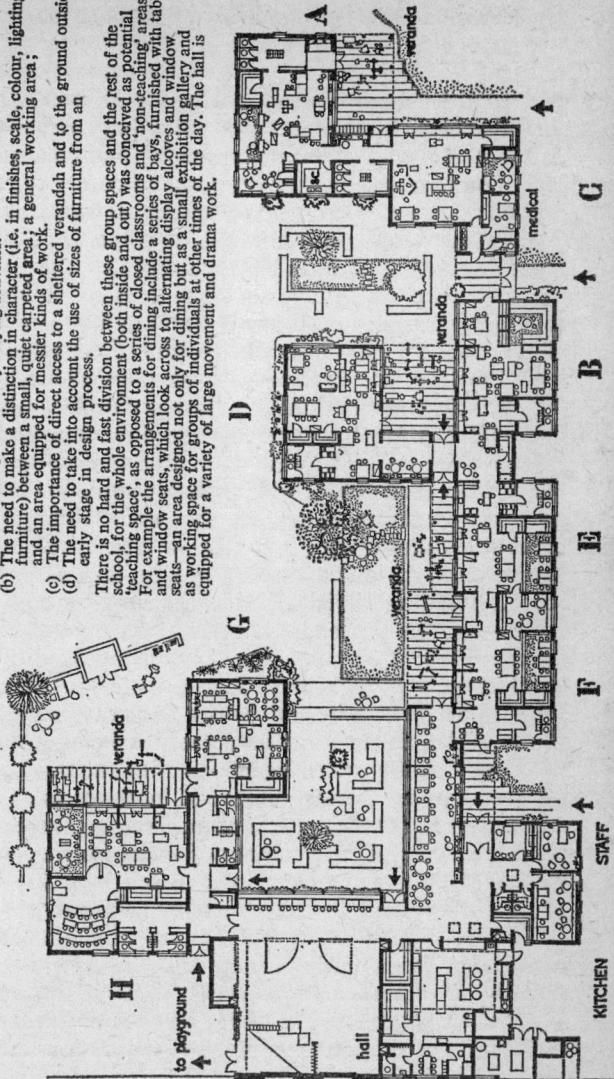

ing attempt by the Toronto School Board to evaluate the effectiveness of these new methods. Their research design is unusual. Broadly, instead of directly comparing open plan with traditional schools and looking for differences, they have graded schools by the level of activity that characterizes them and then looked at the distribution of spatial layouts in their high, medium and low activity level schools. Layouts are described as either 'open plan' or traditional 'egg crate'.

They are well aware, however, that the physical environment does not operate in isolation and that simple stimulus-response relationships do not often present themselves as a solution to complex problems of social policy. Hence, they included attention to the social structure of the schools and the ways in which this interacts with the physical layout.

Let us first consider, though, how 'activity' was measured in this study. A large number of behaviour items which were judged to be relevant to the dimension of activity were compiled. They included, as well as those mentioned below, items such as 'proximity of teacher to nearest child', 'pattern of furniture arrangement', 'number of distinguishable noises'. Measures of these items were taken by time sampling in the schools and then subjected to factor analysis (see E2, F1). The purpose of this procedure is to identify, from the pattern of intercorrelations, any consistent underlying dimensions which characterize the behaviour. The investigators identified one such 'principle component' (which accounted for 60 per cent of the variance) and then used the five items which showed the closest affinity to this component for the main study. The five items were: (a) the number of focal points of activity in a given space, (b) the amount of movement, (c) the number of child 'clusters', (d) the number of social isolates, and (e) the variety of equipment being used. Each item was converted to a scale by giving the scorer a three point range.

This is a good stage, perhaps, at which to remind the reader that factor analysis may point to the existence of an underlying dimension in multiple observations, but the researcher has to endow this with a name and, further, he often uses it (as in this case) as an operational criterion of some special phenomenon in which he is interested.

The authors were confident that their empirically selected 'package' of variables would represent, adequately, the differences between schools in 'activity'. Some might argue that, although the scales represent something coherent, it is not the *essence* of creative learning activity.

To make the point clearer; dispersed, centripetal behaviour (anarchy, in its extreme form!) would score high on Durlak and Lehman's activity scale and, conversely, a self-selected group of children sitting still and discussing a story that had been read to them would score very low. This is not to disparage, but to point out that the essence of creative, child-centred education is elusive and hard to capture and the present activity scale can only be regarded as a useful first approximation.

Once the scale had been developed and refined, it was applied systematically by two observers, who made three trips to twenty spaces in each school every day for a week – with each trip following a different route.

The social structure of the schools was measured by a questionnaire to teachers which asked how much influence to induce changes in the school organization was normally exercised by the head teacher, by the class teacher, by the pupils and the parents respectively.

Of the twelve schools that were studied, the four with the highest activity level were all found to be open-plan and also to have a dispersed authority pattern, i.e. a 'democratic' social structure. Of the four schools with lowest activity, however, three were also open-plan but without the crucial social organization that appears to be necessary to generate the effect. Most of the traditional 'egg crate' built form schools were in the medium activity level. Hence the results are not clear cut – but they do imply that if the building layout and the social structure are compatible, 'open plan' can realize the objectives set for it.

Another important feature of this study is its emphasis on the possibilities for active modification of the building by users who have particular notions about how education should be conducted and who possess a social structure which facilitates their implementation.

Children's playgrounds present the same range of variation between traditional and 'open-plan', the equivalent in the latter case being the so-called 'adventure playground' which contrasts sharply with the more formal play space equipped with fixed steel apparatus of standard design. The provision of play space has become increasingly necessary in urban areas.

A recent study in New York used a variety of methods to compare the activities of children, together with their likes and dislikes in three forms of urban playground: the traditional type, the adventure playground and an intermediary type. It was concluded that, contrary to the widely (and conveniently?) held belief that the creative imagination of children can flourish in any environment, it was, in fact, the opportunities provided that had most influence on the children's play. Apart from their individual stimulus effects, the presence of 'loose' materials that lent themselves to change and combination produced more peer interaction and verbal communication.

Classrooms and study spaces

Sommer (1967) carried out an experiment to test the effects of different classroom environments on the degree of participation in discussion by students – and also to map out the spatial ecology. The project was laudable in that the ongoing activity was directly recorded, but the basic design, involving, as it did, only five discussion groups to represent almost as many experimental conditions, was less dependable. The conditions were a comparison between two conventional and one windowless classroom, a laboratory and two seminar rooms (the latter with horseshoe-shaped seating arrangements).

There are obviously many variables at large here apart from the seating arrangements. Some are quite subtle, such as the different seating postures imposed by the furniture which might influence the students' arousal level, and the perceived 'appropriateness' of the respective rooms. Ecologically, the students generally disposed themselves as far from the tutor as they could, i.e. the back rows filled first in the conventional room and the curve of the horseshoe in the seminar rooms; few students would sit 'alongside' the instructor. (Other studies by Sommer suggest that this would have implied co-orientation or friendliness.) Paradoxically, a higher proportion of the class joined in the discussion in the laboratories, in spite of their highly formal layout – but there was a greater *quantity* of discussion in the seminar rooms. Those sitting directly opposite the tutor in the horseshoe and those sitting in front in the conventional classrooms participated more. But since there had been no *random* allocation to spatial positions (surely the reef on which so many generalizations in environmental psychology have foundered), this was possibly due to self-selection on the part of the more zealous students.

It is very likely that when the choice is voluntary, students take up seating positions according to the relationship they wish to establish with the teacher. Canter (1969) carried out a neat experiment by varying the initial position of the tutor in a relatively neutral situation where students were merely given a questionnaire to complete and then left to choose a seat. In a horseshoe shape arrangement the distance of the tutor made no significant difference, but over eight trials the mean rate of use of 'flanking' positions was only ·8 compared with 3·1 for all other positions. This confirms Sommer's findings.

However, the direct frontal plane from the teacher was avoided, the highest frequencies occurring in an arc of about twenty degrees on each side. Perhaps the optimum position lies at a balance between seeing the tutor clearly and yet not being under his 'straight ahead' scrutiny. A similar explanation can be extended to the trials in a rectangular classroom where distance from the tutor was found to be a very strong determinant, providing we argue that increases in distance act in the same way as obliqueness of direction, i.e. to blunt the teacher's observational acuteness. When he stood 3m from the front row 75 per cent of 'sittings' were in the front three of the total six rows. When he stood 5m away, however, 87 per cent of sittings were in the three back rows.

The concept of personal space has been used by Sommer and others to explain results of this kind but it is hard to see that it has much explanatory as distinct from descriptive power. Most of the seating positions are outside the range which can cause discomfort by implying intimacy; hence, it would seem more parsimonious to say that the spacing is governed by the particular needs of each situation, operating within the constraints set by norms which have evolved within different organizations. The seating norms for bedtime stories, prayer meetings, seminars, lectures and political meetings are all clearly different.

Sommer and Peterson (1967) have done some interesting work on the use of carrels – the small, private, but necessarily cupboard-like enclosures which are sometimes provided in colleges and libraries to facilitate solitary and undisturbed study. In a number of separate studies in American colleges, about half the students who were questioned said they did not find the carrels to be satisfactory environments for work, and when given the chance to design the ideal environment they produced something more like a study/dormitory. It is common experience in these studies and elsewhere that carrels frequently remain unused and students appear to find the presence of others (or the recorded cacophony of contemporary music!) more conducive to work than isolation. The 'social facilitation' and 'audience' experiments referred to earlier are obviously relevant here.

However, Sommer (1970) points out that there is enormous variety in the ecology of student study behaviour depending on personality and on task and situation variables. He gave questionnaires to several thousand students found sitting in libraries, residences, cafeterias, lounges, general classrooms, specialized libraries and outdoor areas. He concluded

> Putting together the results of our interviews and observations, it becomes clear that it is an illusion to think in terms of an 'ideal study environment'. No single study situation, whether it is a library carrel or dormitory room with lounge chairs can satisfy the needs of introverts and extroverts, lone and group studiers, students who must use laboratory or studio equipment, and those who need access to reference materials. What is needed is a variety of study situations that can appeal to students with particular interests. In related surveys, we have found that very little group studying takes place on college campuses, even though many students expressed a desire to do more of it. One reason for infrequent group studying is a lack of quiet places where small groups can get together and work. As we have seen, many students come to the cafeteria for just this reason, but the noise and lack of privacy are distinct disadvantages of a cafeteria setting (p. 277).

Another conclusion that is of growing importance in times of stringency is that considerable scope exists for stage managing spaces for multiple uses. For example, cafeterias can be more effectively used for study than at present and library reading rooms can be separated from book stacks so that they can be used after hours, all night if necessary, by the many students who apparently already study there using their *own* books.

Classroom temperature and pupil performance

The effects on schoolchildren's comfort and work performance of the temperature of the classroom has formed the subject of a variety of studies conducted in climate chambers, specially constructed classrooms and under normal school conditions. Generally, we probably have a better understanding of the thermal environment and its influence on people than of any other group of variables. The effects are not large within the normal range of temperature in buildings, but they are consistent; they are directly measurable using the invaluable approaches that have evolved from classical psychophysics (see A4) and, perhaps most important, their control in buildings is an adequate technology.

With adult subjects, Griffiths and McIntyre (1971) used subjective assessment of comfort derived from large numbers of semantic differential scales (see p. 72). Factor analysis of these scales reveals that they encompass four major axes of sensation; warmth, evaluation, humidity and non-uniformity.

Within a climate chamber, at least, changes in air temperature at a rate as slow as ·5°C per hour are detectable. Humidity can also be directly perceived, though only at the higher temperatures. Indeed, there are important interaction effects between air temperature and humidity, as many literary observations on climate and personality have informed us! At moderate temperatures (23°C) both high and low humidity are judged to be uncomfortable and when it is hotter (28°C) low humidity is preferred.

Another dimension of the thermal environment that has led to theory and speculation is the radiant/convectance one. Mean radiant temperature is the average measure taken from a number of surfaces, i.e. walls, windows, ceilings etc. In modern light-frame buildings there can be large seasonal fluctuation in both positive and negative directions between mean radiant and mean convectance (air) temperature. However, the average experimental subject is apparently insensitive to combinations of these variables (to which differences in quality such as 'freshness', 'stuffiness' etc. have often been ascribed) and it appears that calculable increases in the one will compensate fully for reduction in the other.

Most of the research in schools has taken performance on batteries of tests as the dependent variables. In one well designed experiment, four matched groups of children were placed in one of two virtually identical classrooms and with similar teachers. The 'model' thermal environment in one room had a relatively low temperature, low humidity and high air movement compared with the 'marginal' environment. Normal school routines were followed except for half an hour of experimental testing twice each day.

Differences in the predicted direction were established for a reasoning test, for clerical tasks and for learning new concepts from films – though the latter test did not discriminate significantly between the two environments.

The Climate Group at the National Swedish Institute for Building Research has accumulated extensive research experience in this area. They have shown that in the climate chamber people are more easily distracted by noise at high temperatures and less effective at arithmetical tasks. In a language laboratory, the less able children were adversely affected and in both normal and experimental classrooms many test results were lower in the higher temperatures.

Humphreys (1974) has argued that the testing situation in many thermal environment investigations is artificial, creating altered states of motivation and hence limiting the extent to which results can be generalized to real life. This would seem fair comment if the results were generally negative, because it is well known that human beings can compensate for adverse environments by an extra expenditure of effort. However, the fact that many significant decrements in performance have been found under test conditions suggests that real life conditions may be even more deleterious.

To overcome the problem of such subject 'reactivity', Humphreys first developed an elaborate procedure for collecting teachers' assessments of the effects of hot, wet, cold and windy afternoons on the children in their charge. Fifteen semantic differential scales describing the children's behaviour were completed by teachers and subjected to principal component analysis. The main factor to emerge seemed to be one of 'industriousness' or 'application'; the children being described as settled, willing, responsive, careful and helpful. A second important factor appeared to represent the degree of 'energy' or 'vivacity' of the class; the children being energetic, wide awake, wild, vocal and inquisitive.

Plotting teachers' judgements on these two dimensions for the various climate conditions, showed that cool days are associated with high industriousness but moderate energy; hot days with low energy and low industriousness and windy days with high energy but low industriousness. Wet days produced no consistent expectation.

Of course it can be argued that these are merely the kind of stereotypes for which the teaching profession is renowned. At best they generate a self-fulfilling prophecy. Fortunately, Humphreys rounded off the investigation with some *in situ* recordings of climate which could be correlated with teachers' direct assessments of classroom behaviour on the part of their 7–8 year-old children. The design is not completely watertight, because the teachers were aware that their assessments were being correlated with climate – but they did not know of the general findings and, in any case, ratings collected with the persistence of four times per day for a fortnight are more likely to be made correctly than in accordance with some preconceived stereotype. The results broadly confirmed the findings from the teachers' more general assessments, although the weather was, for once, insufficiently varied for good clear results to emerge.

Disorderly behaviour and school layout

While it is ardently to be hoped that education can be made sufficiently interesting to the majority of children to sustain their motivation, there will always be some who behave in a disorderly fashion, either through boredom, through a deliberate or unconscious wish to disrupt what is happening or both. Thus it is intriguing that Stebbins (1973) has attempted to compare two completely different styles of architectural layout for their effects on disorderliness.

Unfortunately the comparison is seriously confounded by the fact that one style of school occurs in Newfoundland and the other in Jamaica. Differences in, for example, attitudes to education, climate, teaching methods, are almost certain to contribute to the variation, despite the author's assurance to the contrary. He claims that teachers' attitudes towards discipline are similar and that in two schools (one in each culture) where the layout is exceptional in resembling the style of the other culture, disorderliness levels accord more with architecture than with culture.

The Newfoundland schools are of the rectangular block form common in Europe and North America, with the classrooms totally enclosed and issuing into a central hall or hallway, and having only one or two closely monitored exits to the outside world. By contrast, the Jamaica schools have no hallways and allow egress from every classroom into a wide outside space about which buildings are scattered and interspersed with shady trees, the whole allowing considerable scope for concealment.

Often, because of the need for ventilation and partly for economic reasons, there are only low partitions dividing classrooms and at the boundaries unscheduled communications and unauthorized movements occur in abundance. It seems entirely plausible that the school's social system and the climatic conditions, as well as dictating the architecture, are determined or at least reinforced by it.

School size and school location

Problems of educational policy are by no means limited to the classroom environment. Probably one of the most vital questions is *where* schools should be located in the community, although this often seems to be subordinated to the related and highly controversial question of *how large* they should be. It sometimes appears that the answer to the latter question is 'as large as possible' and, in rural areas particularly, it has followed that they must be more and more widely dispersed.

The size of schools
Curiously there is almost no evidence as to optimum size for a school community by criteria such as academic performance or the social satisfactions of staff and pupils. There is, however, an

98

obvious economy of scale in the provision of staff and of expensive facilities such as stage lighting, technical workshops, pottery kilns and so on, all of which would be prohibitively expensive in smaller school units. It could well be thought, however, that these advantages are outweighed by less tangible but more fundamental social assets of the small school such as a sense of involvement in the local community and a more intimate and manageable social group for the children, with more individual relationships to the staff.

In highly urbanized areas, there should be no problem in achieving schools of a reasonable size from a local catchment area. An area, that is, which is small enough to give a sense of belonging to a local community combined with a short journey to school for all the pupils. Recent trends towards the comprehensive school in Britain appear to be going beyond this principle and there is little informed research that could prevent our city schools from becoming as large as New York City High Schools where more than 50 per cent of children attend schools with more than 4,000 pupils. School planners, instead of taking ecological advantage of high density population to put schools closer together, simply increase school size, so that for New York State, for example, there is a correlation of ·78 between degree of urbanization and school size and of ·61 between urbanization and median income for the 63 county areas. Garbarino (1975) who provided this evidence, quotes a number of sources in support of his conviction that large schools are a direct cause of the alienation of relatively affluent American children in 'megalopolis'. But, of course, there are a number of confounding variables involved. The evidence from more direct studies comparing pupil activities in schools of different sizes does, however, provide support for the thesis.

The 'ecological psychology' studies of 'big school and small school'
Barker and his colleagues (Barker and Gump, 1964: Barker, 1968) have applied the techniques of ecological psychology to a comparison between small and large high schools in Kansas. As discussed earlier (Ch. 2), this mainly requires the identification and analysis of 'behaviour settings', i.e. nodes of human activity within a specific geographical location (including its furnishings and other physical props), having a recognizable

beginning and end to a pattern of behaviour which is generally understood by those taking part.

People themselves change as they move from setting to setting and within the same setting, but different people can inhabit the same setting without basically changing its nature.

The average number of people 'manning' a behaviour setting is seen as a crucial ecological variable and within schools (as within many other institutions) it is found that the smaller units tend to have 'undermanned' behaviour settings. Barker and Gump found that 29 per cent of the pupils in large ('over-manned') schools held no positions of importance or responsibility, while the corresponding figure for small schools was only 2 per cent. Furthermore, those who do become involved in small schools with 'optimal manning of behaviour settings' perform in more than twice as many different settings on average, and six times as many of the really important settings, such as team membership and chairmanship of meetings.

The reasons for these differences are made quite explicit in the responses to systematic questioning. There are strong conformity mechanisms for regulating behaviour which Barker labels (a little portentously perhaps) 'deviation-countering feedback (D-mech)'. Children in small schools more often say, for example: 'My teacher talked me into it'; 'They needed girls in the cast'; 'Everyone was supposed to be there'.

Moreover, the data confirmed that involvement is apparently experienced as more satisfying; children are aware of this.

The cynic might say that participation or 'getting involved' is a cult value pursued for its own sake, particularly in the USA. It is true that there is not much direct research evidence to support the assumption that social participation is mentally and socially beneficial; but it is an assumption held so universally among those with direct professional experience that it would seem a sure investment for social policy. Furthermore, the ecological psychologists do provide ample evidence that involvement is at least satisfying to those who engage in it, and the pursuit of individual satisfaction for citizens is one of our widely held social values. The pupils from small high schools report more frequently that they gain satisfaction from 'being challenged', 'being valued', 'gaining moral and cultural values', and 'developing competence'.

100

Educationists (and the parents of children in large public boarding schools) not infrequently point approvingly to the great variety of activities that are provided in large schools. The important paradox indicated by the ecological psychologists is that the larger schools with a greater variety of behaviour settings are likely to be *functionally* more impoverished for the children themselves.

Barker does not refer to the fact that fewer settings must restrict the range of choice that can be exercised by pupils, but even this could be regarded as advantageous, for presumably it is the more socially *basic* settings that survive in small schools and it is these that every child should experience.

The ecology of the rural school

Country schools have always presented the administrator with difficulties because any increase in their size imposes substantially longer school journeys on the children. Nonetheless, mainly between 1930–50 a process named 'reorganization' was implemented in Britain ('consolidation' in the USA). Children of secondary age were removed from their village schools and taken in buses to large schools serving a wide catchment area. As a result, many of the village schools were no longer viable in size as primary schools and had to be closed. This process merged into a related administrative policy, i.e. the grouping of small primary schools into 'area' schools, again by using bus transport but this time for children of age five upwards. This second policy was named 'closure' by country people and has always aroused great hostility.

It is a strange paradox that although compulsory education only began in 1870, the number of schools in Devon, where the research described below was carried out, was reduced by 30 per cent during the period 1900–50, although the population increased by 20 per cent.

Reorganization and rural depopulation. The argument generally advanced by planners is that sparse and declining populations no longer support schools, which then have to be removed. The evidence from a study which related the process of reorganization to rural depopulation (Lee, 1961) is

101

that populations decline partly *because* the schools are removed.

In Devonshire, census population figures for 280 parishes were used to compare population growth and decline during 1931–51 (expressed in relation to a basal growth rate derived from 1911–31) between communities whose schools had been exposed to long and short periods of reorganization. The relative decline was significantly greater as a function of years of exposure. To check the possibility that this correlation was due to some other factor (e.g. that schools in declining areas were singled out for early action), 'early' and 'late' reorganized parishes were matched in pairs on their absolute size, their previous rate of growth and their economic/geographical area. The evidence for a link between period of reorganization and depopulation remains strong. Furthermore, the decline in the 96 parishes which were totally devoid of schools was found to be very severe indeed when compared with the 280 parishes in the sample. The study was later extended to cover the period 1951–61 and the results are shown in Fig. 5.3.

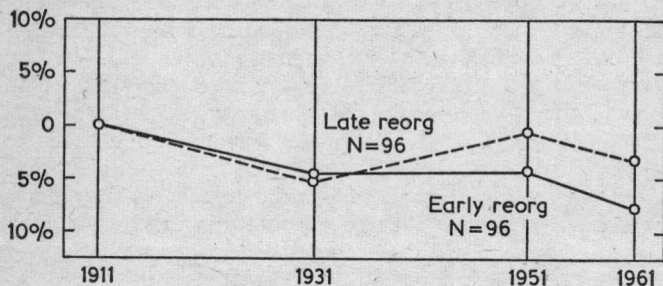

Fig. 5.3 *Based on Lee (1961)*

Effects of school closure on the children
Although there has always been concern in country areas over the ecological effects of educational policies, it is 'closure' and the 'bussing' of young children that has evoked most passion. A study was conducted (Lee, 1957), again in Devon, to investigate the possibility that long school journeys have a directly disturbing effect on young children.

Without being informed in advance of the objectives of

the research, teachers from 57 of the village schools made assessments of their children on ten dimensions of behaviour in school. The sample were aged mainly 6 and 7 years but with a small subsample of 8-year-olds; the total number was 883.

The behaviour dimensions were measures of social and emotional adjustment such as 'aggressiveness', 'general anxiety', 'concentration', 'energy', 'response to affection' etc., and almost all these showed a consistent effect when related to the length and type of school journey. When standardized and combined into an overall index of *adjustment*, the picture was even clearer (Fig. 5.4).

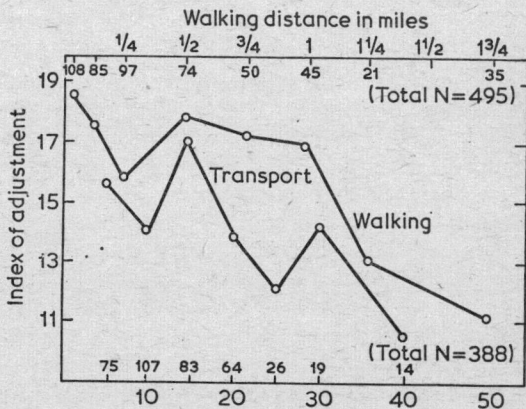

Fig. 5.4 *From Lee (1957) (N.B. High score is equivalent to 'good' adjustment)*

As the length of both walking and bussing journeys increases, there is a corresponding deterioration in the social adjustment of the child in the school. Thus far, it confirms the anxiety of the mothers who have claimed that the long journeys are excessively demanding for very young children.

However, the surprising result was that, for roughly equal journey times, travel in the school bus was found to have consistently more damaging effects than walking. This can hardly be explained by a simple fatigue hypothesis. The explanation that comes closest to fitting the data (including the facts that boys are more adversely influenced than girls; and that with age the effect on both sexes of walking journeys levels off but not the effect of bus journeys) is a psychological one.

Young children have extremely limited 'inner representations' of geographical space. They form a 'schema' of the home and home range and of the school environment in which they spend so much time. If they have to walk to school, the journey comprises a *barrier*; but depending on its length, it is not too serious an obstacle because the children's direct daily contact with the environment of paths, lanes, fields and landmarks, constantly articulated by their own voluntary route decisions, means that they build a 'causeway schema' connecting these two vital behaviour settings. They know that the barrier between them can fairly easily be surmounted at any time, and the mother, at the heart of the child's world, can be reached whenever he wishes.

The bussing child, by contrast, is relatively severed from the home for long periods each day. He acquires no effective 'causeway schema' because his attention is mainly taken up by the inside of the bus and he has no involvement whatever in the route decisions. Furthermore, when the steel container deposits its young passengers at the school, it disappears for the remainder of the day, often leaving no effective connection at all. Hence, it is argued that the spatial ecology may be a cause of intermittent daily maternal separation anxiety which in some circumstances may have escalating effects.

It is extremely difficult for adults to comprehend such phenomena because they anthropomorphize, i.e. they attribute to children a spatial understanding similar to their own, because they so easily confuse this personal, elaborately constructed 'inner representation' with reality; with what is actually 'out there'. We assume that it is automatically available to all because it is there for us.

6
The design of hospitals

The physical environment of a hospital can probably make a substantial contribution to the patient's well-being and hence to his recovery. This is obvious insofar as the complex social machinery of administrators, doctors, nurses, cleaners and functional specialists can communicate better and integrate their complex tasks to reach these goals more effectively; less obvious is the fact that a well planned hospital can minimize the inevitable feeling of disorientation, the separation from familiar routines and from the personal interdependencies that give a meaningful context to the personality. These considerations are magnified for specialist hospitals such as those designed for maternity, child or mental patients, and these groups have accordingly received the most research attention.

Time and space in a maternity hospital

A maternity hospital is an extreme example of a purpose-built space for the rapid repetition of a complex production process. A social organization with various professional roles and large differences in status attempts to maintain a working rhythm of production, most of it conventional, but with important contingency arrangements. Consequently, the layout of the building is closely patterned to the social tasks.

This interdependency was studied by Rosengren and De

Vault (1963) in a large hospital in the USA, catering for both publicly supported and private patients. They used the method of 'participant observation', dressing in hospital uniform and gradually acquiring an unobtrusive and generally accepted role. Much of their observation was concerned with the ways in which the hospital team attempted to regulate the temporal rhythm within a situation where the number of births could vary from one or two to twenty per day. However, we are more concerned with the ecology, which, as the authors say, '... was intimately in exchange with many of the salient social processes of the hospital'.

The admitting office has no doors or barriers of any kind and is characterized by friendly casualness and informal dress. It is a 'transitional space'. The 'prep room', on the other hand, is a place where the patient is depersonalized and turned into a medical case; a number of routines take place there that are mundane by contrast with the traumatic apotheosis which is to later take place in the delivery room. As with other lowly functions, 'preparation' is removed to a separate place and its overseers are the lower status personnel, particularly student nurses. The labour room has a strong shoulder-high barrier separating both nurses in charge and patients from all other passers by, and apparently reinforcing the separation of the somewhat higher status group of nurses, who were autonomous within its symbolic confines. This barrier also served to define a 'back stage area' (Goffman, 1959) where they could let their hair down among themselves and depart from the strict enactment of formal roles required in more public situations (see B2). Equivalent spaces exist for the housemen ('interns') and for the senior consultants (the 'pros'). These were strongly separated by physical barriers from the other circulation spaces, and in the latter case strongly personalized, relatively luxurious and largely devoid of any intrusion from the production processes. The housemen's room, by contrast, has a large scoreboard on which deliveries are recorded and monitored.

The recovery rooms and most particularly the 'fathers' room' are also subordinate to the delivery room.

The 'fathers' room' is adjacent to the recovery room – unattended and suggestive that the father is regarded as the least important person in the process. By its sparseness of

106

furnishing, its physical isolation and its small size, the room seemed to communicate symbolically the idea that the father was unnecessary and functionally peripheral.

It is in the delivery room that the consultant reigns supreme – where the real 'business' is done. But whatever the physiological indications, no patient reaches there without being duly sequenced through the full ecological route. If there seem sometimes to be urgent grounds for shortcutting, these indications tend to be 'reconstrued' by the staff. Even more intriguing is the phenomenon that must surely be confirmed by many mothers. There is an imposed ecology of pain, i.e. if pain is expressed in the admission room, in the 'prep room' or even in the labour ward it tends to be redefined by all concerned, including the patient, unless its degree of severity conforms with the accepted gradient as the delivery room is approached. It is only at this high altar that severe pain is really sanctioned, nay expected, and a special high grade functionary in the form of the anaesthetist is ready to deal with it appropriately.

The formal roles and their accorded status are thus elaborately maintained not only by the culture but by the ecological framework and by the manifold symbolism of physical instruments, uniform etc. Even the patients, relatively depersonalized as they are, share in this. For example, the privacy of a closed door to a delivery room is accorded only to private patients, who also enjoy the relative anonymity of a room number instead of the familiar name that is used for low status, publicly supported patients.

Some of the obvious dangers of a social system in which roles are acted out somewhat inflexibly in public are mitigated by 'back stage' readjustments, and it is notable that the environment again helps to legitimate this process. The normal taboos against mutual criticism across roles are lifted in the interstitial areas, such as hallways and corridors, and even in the cafeteria: 'Here the doctor, nurse, intern and student nurse may be found speaking together in the most candid fashion.'

Many of the mechanisms described by Rosengren and De Vault undoubtedly operate unconsciously, and the pattern of social behaviour derives from the interaction of a well-established medical culture with the environmental framework in subtle ways that cannot possibly be unravelled by these observational-type approaches. The medical culture, however, has been nurtured in similar buildings and will impose its pattern on future buildings. The two have a similar and mutually reinforcing structure because they have evolved together to achieve certain goals. If this is made explicit to both users and architects in the briefing process, then the mutual compatibility can be improved; but even more important, if there is a change of emphasis in the goals towards, for example, a more personalized or a more family-oriented childbirth service – then a redesign of the building layout could be expected to help in the modification of the new social system. For example, to anticipate the discussion later in this chapter, most children's hospitals have been based on the conventional assumption that the ward units should each deal with different illnesses, whereas the design team of a new hospital in Palo Alto has differentiated according to children's age – on the grounds that there is greater variety between children at different stages in their development than between children with different disorders. This is a radical departure that might detract from the efficiency of the more technological aspects but which could also have less obvious treatment benefits.

Basic floor plans in a general hospital

There are advocates for three alternative basic floor plans for wards (nursing units) in the design literature on hospitals. It is obviously desirable that their relative strengths and weaknesses should be assessed, since medical routines have a high degree of standardization and are reproduced in thousands of hospitals throughout the world. The most common layout is the *single corridor*, usually linear or L-shaped, with the nursing station at the centre or angle; secondly there is the *double corridor*, each one serving beds or rooms along one edge and with the other services spread along between them; and finally, the *radial* has a nursing station at the centre with rooms encircling it.

So far as nursing work-loads are concerned, similar considerations presumably apply whether the beds are in single rooms or open plan.

The Rochester Methodist Hospital in Minnesota has been deliberately built in a way to allow such experimental comparison and Trites and his colleagues (1970) were able to collect data on no less than four examples of each design within the same hospital. Understandably, it was not possible to match the type of cases or to balance the physician/nurse teams across wards (see A8), but this was overcome by using a statistical technique for controlling 'interfering' variables, such as the intensity of nursing care needed for different types of case. Each ward had three shifts of personnel, which virtually gave three independent replications of the experiment. A total of 77,400 observations were made of 590 staff.

There are two main groups of dependent variables in the experiment. The first consisted of sixteen measures of the type and location of nurses' activity, using work study methods. These data were collected by time sampling, i.e. observers made rounds at predetermined intervals and coded what each member of the work team was doing, and where. Secondly, each member completed a questionnaire before and after each of his work shifts and from these, fourteen measures of subjective feeling were derived along such dimensions as fatigue, anxiety, perceptions of work-load etc.

The results of the work study analyses showed that the radial design was significantly superior to the double corridor and this in turn better than the single corridor. Staff on the radial ward spent less time on travel and more time with their patients. Despite this, they were more often to be found working in the nursing station and to be engaged in non-productive activity.

The massive questionnaire study on subjective feelings of staff turned out to be inconclusive, but two supplementary studies lent further support. The level of absenteeism and the number of accidents may both be considered indirect measures of nurses' response, and both these significantly favoured the radial design. Finally, a 'natural' experiment occurred when medical and surgical services were interchanged between the radial and double corridor design. The large majority of both patients and staff who were interviewed preferred the radial and judged that it endowed a higher quality of patient care.

109

In a general hospital, speed and efficiency are obviously of prime importance, but it is to be hoped that future studies at Rochester will extend to include aspects of the social context of the alternative ward designs. It is common knowledge, for example, that many patients prefer to 'see what is going on', and research has shown that walking patients cluster wherever they can find a suitable place for 'company' and a 'gossip'. These satisfactions would justify certain design characteristics in their own right, but they may also have therapeutic value – a more intangible question but one that turns up in many environmental policy decisions. It is in *mental* hospitals, however, that it assumes pre-eminence and it is to these that we will next turn attention.

The mental hospital

More than half of all hospital beds are psychiatric or geriatric, the staffing ratio is exceedingly low and the buildings, though often in beautiful settings, are old and gloomy.

Perhaps an extreme example is reported by Spivak (1967) from the United States. As an observer relatively unfamiliar with such institutions he circulated through mental hospitals, setting down his impressions. Most of the time was spent in endless corridors, one of them 2,970 feet long, which had monotonous reflecting paint surfaces and few relieving features. The walls were also highly sound reflective, causing echoes and strange other-worldly effects. He claims to have experienced visual distortions of other people, such as 'fuzzy outlines', pinching of ankles, wrists and neck. If these effects seem more dramatic than average (and it must be remembered that considerable effort has been put into brightening up over the past two decades) they should at least serve as a sharp reminder that many mental patients spend their lives in a confused struggle on the borderlands of reality, and if their environment is characterized by unfamiliarity, depersonalization and monotony, they are more likely to lose this battle (see F3).

Many writers agree that the patients in mental hospitals need clearly-defined spaces, but not so varied in function that they are a source of confusion. They need areas of visual and acoustic privacy, and they are often difficult to convince that these are achieved with glass partioning. Nonetheless, patients with anxiety symptoms will frequently be unhappy in rooms which have only one exit or which are disproportionately large, such as institutional type dining rooms. The repetition of identical elements such as windows, doors, check floor tiles and monotonous sounds such as humming fans or ticking clocks tend to cause disturbance. In many hospitals, privacy is invaded by the removal of personal possessions or by the imposition of 'rights to inspect', which of course extend to the patient's own body. There are sometimes no doors on the lavatories.

There have been several empirical studies of the social relationships which form among schizophrenic patients, in particular. An early example involved two methods of observation. Firstly, charting positions, activities and postures of each patient at given time intervals by reference to a floor grid plan. Secondly, recording individual patients continuously on the same measures for up to ten hours.

The aim was to explore the relationship between the social dominance of patients and their territorial behaviour. It was found that the most dominant ones used the whole ward as their territory, a middle group were often to be found in high traffic positions where they could extend their social contacts, and the low status ones had definite 'hideaway places'.

However, since the definition of social dominance seemed hard to distinguish from sociability, the relationship is almost tautologous. Also, the more dominant patients may have been found to be just as dependent on their territories if the study had been cast on a wider spatial range. Later studies in homes for maladjusted boys have given conflicting answers to this question, and perhaps all it is safe to assert at present is that a range of territorial needs and behaviour will be found among patients. This is redolent of Horowitz et al's (1964) notion of the 'body buffer zone' – the distance which a person preserves around the body as inviolate, or at least into which intrusions cause discomfort. He found that patients would normally approach less closely to people than to inanimate objects (he used a hatstand!) and male patients less closely to other males than to females. Schizophrenic patients were found to have larger body buffer zones than depressives and neurotics. It is

111

particularly important that this measure could be used to chart any progress they made. For example, one group of schizophrenics preserved a mean distance of 42 inches soon after admission, which was reduced to 25 inches on a later trial.

Bedroom occupancy in psychiatric wards

One of the most important design decisions that influences behaviour on a psychiatric ward appears to be the number of patients assigned to the bedrooms. Ittelson, Proshansky and Rivlin (1964) concluded this from a behaviour mapping study of psychiatric wards in three large hospitals. The coding categories they used were 'traffic', 'social', 'mixed activities', 'isolated activities' and 'isolated passive'. These were coded in a matrix against public rooms and bedrooms. They found considerable consistency of the patterns over time within hospitals but large differences between hospitals, which were probably attributable to the social class composition of the patient samples. Also, two otherwise similar wards in a State hospital, which had quite different treatment regimes, reflected this in different patient behaviour patterns.

However, the authors were primarily interested in patterns of sufficient generality to manifest themselves across the full range of wards and hospitals. Such was the relationship between bedroom size and behaviour. The proportion of 'isolated passive' behaviour increases regularly with room size (and consequently with the number of persons sharing the room). In two of the hospitals, the correlation is 1.00 and over the whole sample, .60. A reduction in activity (including social interaction) when more people are sharing a room seems paradoxical, especially in the light of the fact that the total amount each person spends in the bedroom remains much the same regardless of its size. What happens, it seems, is that the patients have a tacit understanding not to intrude upon each other and only when a bedroom's capacity is as high as 6 beds or larger is there likely to be more than one person occupying it simultaneously.

However, whether it is the volume of the room or the actual or threatened presence of others that is responsible, the patients occupying larger rooms apparently feel constrained in what they can do. Instead of 'busying' themselves, they spend most of their informal allocation of time lying on the bed, asleep or awake. Furthermore, this is not compensated by an increase in active behaviour while they are in public rooms.

An experiment conducted in one of the hospitals demonstrated that these patterns of behaviour could be modified by deliberate intervention. Immediately following one set of observations, a sun lounge was provided with extra comfortable and attractive furniture, laid out in ways conducive to good conversation. One month later, when behaviour mapping was repeated, the sun lounge's share of total social activity in public rooms had increased from 25 to 42 per cent. Among the readjustments was a drop in 'isolated passive' behaviour in the corridors from 32 to 5 per cent.

This confirms an earlier study of friendships in a mental hospital which showed that patients found in corridors were the friendless ones, followed by those in dormitories, with those in the day room being the friendliest. The conclusion drawn was that corridors encourage social isolation and should be eschewed in future hospital designs, but more work is needed in this important area before we can reliably assume a direct causal link.

Holahan and Saegert (1973) have recently set a good example by allocating patients at random to two basically identical wards, one of which had been extensively refurbished and remodelled with partitioned bedrooms and seating areas. Direct observation and interviews with patients showed that there is significantly more social interaction and less passive behaviour on the new ward. However, although this is encouraging it does not begin to match the standards of evidence expected in other areas of psychology, which would point to the likelihood of confounding by the 'Hawthorne effect', a change in social attitudes arising from sheer involvement in an experiment (see E5).

Research in a Glasgow children's hospital

Canter (1972) has made a comprehensive study of a newly built children's hospital, York Hill, Glasgow. This was presented as a 'building appraisal' and hence its findings are not intended to generalize beyond the particular package of variables combined in a single hospital. Nevertheless, the environmental psychologist has, as pointed out earlier, an extremely important potential role in extending the traditional building appraisal (normally a 'walk about' by an expert) into a systematic survey of user satisfactions and behaviour. Also, there is much to be gained from this study about strategies and methods for hypothesis-testing studies.

First, Kelly's (1955) personal construct theory approach was used to explore the ways in which the hospital as a physical/social organism was 'construed' by the architect and by the senior nursing officer. The elements were the different parts of the hospital, e.g. cardiology, x-ray, admission wards, etc. and these were printed on cards so that the method of 'triads' (in what important way are two of these places similar but different from the third) was used to elicit the 'constructs' (personal modes of construing the hospital environment) of the subjects. The repertory grid method then consists in the presentation of a matrix with the elements along one dimension and the elicited constructs along the other, so that the subject can assess each element numerically on each construct.

From this it is possible, even with a single subject, to calculate the affinities (i.e. correlations) between the different constructs and different elements and across elements and constructs. Then one can display these as a pattern of individual construing. This is done by putting them in two dimensional space, following the simple rule that parts of the hospital (elements) and modes of construing them (constructs) that are positively correlated will be placed correspondingly close and negatively correlated ones correspondingly distant.

The configurations produced in this way are reproduced in Fig. 6·1. They say that the architect in this case has a well balanced set of constructs, encompassing the different physical elements he has designed. This is indicated by the fact that they are not bunched or arranged linearly (which would have indicated differences in degree of one major construct) by contrast with the balanced array, each distinct of its kind. The constructs themselves are concerned with the degree of servicing, difficulty of design, importance of position and so on.

The construing of the senior nursing officer has a similar structure but its content is concerned much more with

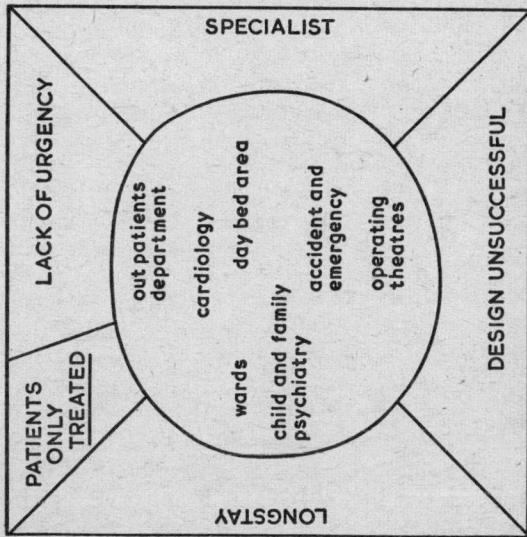

Schematic representation of senior nursing officer's conceptions of the hospital

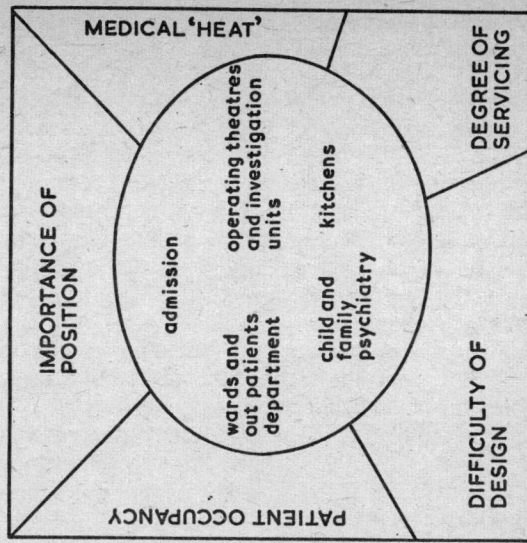

Schematic representation of architects conceptions of the hospital

Fig 6.1 *From Canter (1972)*

patient/staff relations, urgency of treatment, length of stay, etc.

Although the applications of these methods are in their infancy, Canter indicates their potential in a number of different ways. Firstly, we can compare the ways in which the architect sees the building with the user's own conceptions. In the present case, for instance, the senior nursing officer groups cardiology with the day bed area and outpatients because they share in common a lack of urgency in patient treatment, whereas the architect links cardiology with the operating theatres and investigation units because of the high degree of technical servicing involved.

Comparisons can also be made between these repertory grid configurations and other observational data. The architect saw the accommodation for 'staff changing' as quite unrelated to other elements (the senior nursing officer, however, integrated it fully), and this may partly explain the low satisfaction ratings it was given.

The average degree of satisfaction with different parts of the building that was expressed by consultants, nurses, administrators and 'rooming in' mothers identified a number of areas of difference as well as giving a comparative picture of this criterion of the success of different design aspects.

This aspect of the study was extended to a general measure of user satisfaction employed in six other notable buildings in Scotland. Most parts of the hospital scored very highly against these norms, but again, the 'staff changing' area was assessed on average at the absolute bottom of the list.

The hospital occupies a commanding site and members of the public were asked to give their opinion of its appearance. Their approval was positively related to their knowledge of the hospital; being low if they did not recognize it at all, or know it to be a hospital, higher if they had been told it was a hospital and still higher if they recognized it as York Hill. This is a good example of the complex nature of aesthetic appreciation and the unreality of considering it in pure terms, i.e., in isolation from a knowledge of a person's functional evaluation of the building. It is significant that of forty-five subjects who had no initial recognition of the building, only two, when asked to guess, judged it to be a hospital. Nearly half thought it was a university, and of these it was the ones who were in-

Average scores when 102 respondents were asked to indicate how each part of the ward listed on left rated for each description below by putting the appropriate number from 1—7 in the box alongside

	EASY TO GET TO FROM MOST OTHER PARTS OF THE WARD 1 for difficult—7 for easy	CAN USUALLY SEE CHILDREN THERE EASILY 1 for with difficulty—7 for easily	EASY TO NURSE IN 1 for difficult—7 for easy	USUALLY A PLEASANT PLACE TO BE 1 for unpleasant—7 for pleasant	SUITABLE FOR CHILDREN 1 for not really suitable—7 for suitable	QUIET 1 for too noisy—7 for quiet	HOMELY 1 for clinical—7 for homely	VIEW OUT 1 for bad—7 for good	SPACE 1 for cramped—7 for spacious
Day space (playroom)	5·31	3·46	4·67	6·28	6·30	3·99	5·59	6·26	5·98
Six-bed bay	5·83	4·68	5·98	6·10	6·04	4·50	4·56	5·84	6·28
Treatment	5·80	3·41	5·41	4·31	4·90	5·44	2·27	2·44	5·45
Parent/child cubicles	5·42	3·80	5·60	5·72	5·32	5·49	4·69	4·24	4·91
Nurses station	6·32	5·55	4·75	5·50	4·33	4·03	3·72	3·66	5·04
Four-bed bay	6·35	6·12	6·14	6·03	6·05	4·74	4·03	5·39	6·10
Preparation room	5·90	3·67	4·45	4·84	3·99	4·85	2·64	2·45	5·19
Doctors' room	4·31	2·63	3·34	4·45	3·31	5·36	3·47	3·36	5·18
Bathroom	5·78	3·59	4·77	5·23	5·67	4·47	4·65	2·26	5·50
Sisters' room	4·70	2·38	3·33	4·97	3·19	5·68	3·87	3·77	5·40

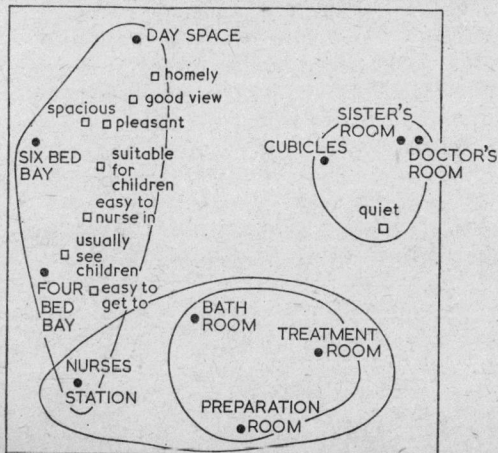

Fig. 6.2 *From Canter (1972)*

formed of its true function who thought best of its visual appearance.

A repertory grid approach was applied to the various parts of the wards and in this case, the results were averaged for 102 subjects. Both the questionnaire and the configuration are shown in Fig. 6.2. In this case there is a noticeably linear dimension which appears to underlie all but one of the nine constructs. It may be described as a 'functional-homely' dimension with aspects of nursing efficiency ('usually see the children') at one end and 'homely', 'spacious', 'pleasant', at the other. Most revealing, however, is that while the nurses' station and the day space are obviously at opposite poles, the six-bed bays are seen as more homely and suitable for children while the four-bed bays are more functionally efficient.

The cubicles are in a totally separate grouping with the doctors' and sister's rooms and it is this area alone, it seems, that is characterized by quietness.

Canter's study includes further sections on the appraisal of wards by sisters and of the hospital experience by 'rooming-in' mothers. Also, behavioural mapping was used to examine the patterns of usage of space on the wards.

Although the methods still need a good deal of refinement, this kind of sympathetic and comprehensive approach to all the major user groups of a building, employing a variety of measurement techniques, could not fail to lead to an improvement in the design process. If more widely adopted, it could help in the evolution of the building as it is adapted over time, and the feedback can help the individual architect to know his strength as well as his weaknesses, provide invaluable input for the training of new architects, and improve the briefing of ones who are inexperienced with a particular building type. It would seem a more rational way of profiting from experience than the present methods of ultimate survival of the successful and of learning by successive expensive error.

The cost of appraising a hospital in this way is a miniscule proportion of the total capital and recurrent budget.

7
The maze of the city

Contemporary approaches to behaviour in cities have diverged along two main paths. On the one hand there are the inheritors of the urban ecological tradition, established by the Chicago School of sociologists of the 1920s. Their method is to take objective measurements of behaviour, either directly, or more commonly through demographic statistics, and to show how these are related to spatial dimensions. The second method has its roots in cognitive maps, imagery and Lewin's notion of 'life space' and may be described as the subjective or 'phenomenal' approach. It is the second of these that has come to be regarded as the distinctive approach of environmental psychology and to which most attention will therefore be given here. But it is certainly not the only one, and objective studies of behaviour at the city scale are also grist to its mill.

Before considering the direct empirical studies, however, there are two traditional research areas in psychology that cast some light on the ways in which people conceptualize the city. These are maze learning and imagery.

Maze learning

How do we find our way about? Attempts were made to answer this question during the 1930s and 1940s in two apparently different ways. Both were based on experiments with

119

rats in mazes. Hull (1943) claimed that correct *movements* in response to stimuli from different parts of the environment are learned, to the extent that they are reinforced (rewarded) by bringing the animal nearer to the goal. Tolman (1932) averred that the *environment itself* is learned and that the rat can employ any of a wide range of movements to take him where he wants to go, i.e. towards rewarding places.

The *cross maze* provided powerful evidence in the controversy. Rats who had learned to turn left at the 'cross roads' to reach their food were started from the opposite end of the maze to see if they would reproduce the well-learned left turn, or whether they would 'know' that the food was now over on the right. They did. In other mazes, when a well-learned direct route to the goal was blocked, rats chose the next shortest route, although they had experienced no direct reinforcement at the choice points involved. In the famous 'sunflower maze' they showed that if a well-learned path whose first turn leads away from the goal is removed and replaced by a series of paths radiating in all directions, they can choose the one that heads for the goal although it points in a direction opposite to all their initial learning.

A series of experiments on 'latent learning' (see A3) showed that movement responses in the maze do not need to be reinforced for learning to occur. Rats learned a great deal by simply being left overnight in a maze without a goal box at all. This knowledge was not apparent until food was introduced the following day and then the rats soon showed that they knew their way about.

Not all studies of the maze eschewed the human subject. For example, Perrin (1914) compared performance on a full size maze in an amusement park with a stylus maze of the same design. His subjects' first glimmer of learning seemed to be a rough knowledge of the position of the exit in relation to the starting point. There is a reminder here of a later study that showed how women first orient to a city by extending the home and neighbourhood out towards the city centre and men by extending the centre back towards the home.

Perrin's subjects described how they had attempted to concentrate either on a visual image of the pattern, a verbal sequence of directions or just a direct feeling about how to move. In fact, all three became variously implicated. This anticipates work with rats in which the sense organs were sequentially removed without identifying any single mechanism on which the animals' spatial cognitions seem to depend. Having learned to run a maze, the poor creatures still demonstrated a mastery of its intricacies when they were required to swim through it (i.e. using totally different motor responses), having had their whiskers, eyes and organs of smell excised and a number of sensory motor neural pathways severed. It seems that inputs from a variety of sensory modes are simultaneously enregistered in the central nervous system, probably in a single model located in the occipital area of the cortex (see A2).

Rats, and men in particular, have a vast complex of factors mediating between stimulus and response and these become uniquely organized into dynamic cognitive structures. Tolman was more aware than most of this and in 1948 he published a brilliant paper summarizing his views and entitled 'Cognitive maps in rats and men'.

It would be a mistake to presume that Tolman won hands down though. Stimulus-response and cognitive learning are probably both implicated in spatial orientation at different stages, and should never have been posed against each other. They constitute the abstraction of a complex process at two successive stages of its establishment; and also the choice of alternative sized units of behaviour. Molar, large-scale units are formed from molecular ones. While the molar approach is obviously more expedient for studying the environment, it is silly to argue from this that S–R psychologists are misguided. Their methods are infinitely more appropriate in some situations; for example, in shaping the spatial behaviour of a child who does not know the way to his mouth with a spoonful of food.

Imagery

The cognitive map provides us with the link between maze learning and imagery. The 'cognitive map' or 'socio-spatial schema' is a hypothetical construct; i.e. we infer its existence from observed behaviour and from introspective reports. Little is known of its neurophysiology beyond an approximate idea of where it is stored in the cortex. The form or forms in which it is coded for storage are not yet understood. However, the experience of retrieving it is, of course, the process of imagery.

Over the years, psychologists have been distinctly fickle with the concept of imagery, but it is currently enjoying respectability (see A6). The beginnings of the affair go back to Galton, a century ago. He asked subjects to evoke an image of their breakfast table and to answer questions about its brightness, clarity and colour. However, the early evidence was largely introspective and was ruled inadmissible by behaviourists.

It is the cognitive psychologists who have reinstated imagery in recent years. Neisser, for example, has asked how preverbal children and animals could possibly learn without some kind of inner pictorial representation and has carried out a number of experiments to show that adults retain and use the capacity for appropriate purposes. Bruner has distinguished the 'iconic' stage of learning which, developmentally, follows the 'enactive' and precedes the 'symbolic' (see C2).

A number of studies have confirmed the reality in some children (one study estimated about 8 per cent) of *eidetic* imagery. This is a particularly vivid form of image which the subject 'sees' as if projected on to a plain external surface. In adults there are large individual differences in the vividness of normal imagery. It is a mistake to suppose that it consists simply in the reproduction of representations which resemble more or less faded photographs. On the contrary, images are generally reported as patchy, uneven to the point of having large gaps, fluctuating and shifting. Sequences of images are capable of being 'run past a window in the mind'.

Bartlett (1932) was particularly influential in stressing the role of imagery in memory and in the processes of recognition. His notion of the 'schema' was an active synthesis of sensations as well as a template (or, in computer parlance, a 'programme') for action. This is also the sense in which Piaget uses the concept. E. J. Gibson (1969) has emphasized that man is not a passive receptacle and pigeonholer of sensations which fuse together to form static images. On the contrary, he actively scans and continually seeks to analyse external stimuli. His aim is to detect their distinguishing characteristics, in order to articulate the inner representations and so enable him to differentiate one external object from another. This emphasis on the *constructive* nature of perception and memory that is stressed by the cognitive psychologists also owes a great deal to Bartlett, who showed empirically how the schema underwent both 'levelling' of its invariant features and 'sharpening' of distinctive elements, the latter as a result of attention to particular details which had special functional significance for the subject. The relevance of this to 'imaging' the city is obvious.

Verbal mediators or 'labels for things' are undoubtedly used over a very wide range of cognitive processing, particularly in our own highly literate society. But however widespread the phenomenon of acoustic encoding, it has been shown that children below about five do not show the homophonic disadvantage (confusing say 'hat' and 'bat' in memory even when they are presented as pictures) and it is therefore far from universal. Obviously a great deal depends on the nature of the stimulus material and it is evident that a wide range of spatial-environmental experience simply does not lend itself to verbal coding.

A good example is a study by Start and Richardson (1964) who taught their subjects a new Olympic high jump technique by giving daily practice through imagery alone. They found that when the performance itself was tested, those who had been found on independent measures to have more controllable and vivid imagery had 'learned' to jump better.

Another line of research that has strongly confirmed the role of imagery in learning has used instructions to evoke images as mediators in paired associate learning (see A6). For example, in learning the word pair zebra–glass as one in a list of apparently meaningless pairings, the subject is encouraged to form an image that connects the two, such as a zebra seated in the stalls of a theatre holding a pair of opera glasses to his eyes (Paivio, 1971). Spatial memories often involve word–place associations. Shepard has devised an ingenious task involving the imaginary folding of an outline shape on paper into a three-dimensional cube (see Shepard and Metzler, 1971). The subject has to report whether two arrows on the flat form would be in juxtaposition on the cube. The time he takes to arrive at a decision for different versions correlates with the actual number of 'folds' needed to make each cube manually.

This is a crucial demonstration because it is inconceivable that the task could be done by verbal or mathematical means.

Altogether, there now seems to be powerful evidence that much of our multi-sensory spatial learning is compiled into some form of inner representation such as a cognitive map or schema and accessed by means of pictorial type imagery. This is not to suggest that verbal mediators are not used at all. Indeed, the importance of much recent research has been in showing that the severe limitation of images is that each is tied to an individual stimulus object or class of objects, and images representing *relationships between objects* are formed only with difficulty. If they could be generated they would constitute, of course, *'relational concepts'*, but it is words that excel in representing these. This assertion can be verified by attempting to evoke 'image groupings' corresponding to and capable of performing the same function as spatial concept words like 'wide', 'high', 'squarish', 'elongated'.

This kind of relational concept is, of course, very different from an *object* concept – a distinction that is insufficiently recognized (see A7). A succession of images formed from a set of similar objects can very well be fused into a composite image – and this is the essence of the 'schema' which is so vital to spatial cognition.

Images of the city

The work of Kevin Lynch (1960) is certainly the best known study of city imagery. Although by no means the first to adopt a subjective, phenomenal approach, his study caught the imagination of other urban designers and it has had a profound influence.

His method was to elicit the images held by middle and upper class residents of three cities; Boston, Los Angeles and Jersey City. This was done both by sketch maps and by a process of questioning, the latter partly while he walked about the city with his subjects. Lynch's aim was to capture the essential character of cities, the structure and identity of meanings formed by constant interaction and serving as a cognitive map to make orientation possible. He pointed to the recurring importance of certain elements; *districts*, with roughly agreed boundaries; *landmarks*, such as the Empire State Building and the Rockefeller Centre; *paths*, i.e. major roads and pedestrian routes which form connections between landmarks; and *nodes* which occur at the intersections of different transportation routes. The emphasis is on the 'image-ability' or 'legibility' of the city. But despite the seminal influence of this work, it has to be admitted that it does not yet lend itself very readily to the solution of practical problems of town planning, and its popularity in schools of design may have been due to its basically *aesthetic* orientation.

Methodologically, the number of subjects was small and hardly representative. The difficult problem of aggregating the images is resolved in part by mapping the elements with varying degrees of prominence and showing paths and boundaries with different thicknesses according to the proportion of subjects for whom they are salient. However, it remains to convey the basic *form* of the 'citizen's image' of the city and for this we have to rely on a subjective synthesis formed by the investigator himself.

Appleyard (1970) extended Lynch's methods in his study of Cuidad Guayana, Venezuela, using larger samples and making possible a comparison of different kinds of maps that tended to be associated with different educational levels. The less mobile working class residents drew predominantly strip maps, with gross distortions of the areas remote from the main linear route. Only their own neighbourhoods were articulated in detailed, two-dimensional terms. Middle and upper class people perceived their neighbourhoods to be significantly more remote from slum areas than is actually the case.

De Jonge (1962) compared the images of Rotterdam, Amsterdam and The Hague. Amsterdam emerges as the most legible of cities because of its unique spider web pattern of concentric canals, related to a very strong linear core, including the Central Station and a great square containing the Royal Palace. He presents quantitative evidence that people use the road system as a basic framework if it is legible, but otherwise compose their city images around the anchor points of major landmarks.

The dilemma of these studies is nicely demonstrated by a comparison made by De Jonge of two residential districts. One is highly legible because of its uniform ground plan and

125

the other distinctly baffling because of its almost random connections and the deceiving curves of its roadways. The latter, however, was much preferred. He concludes, '... an area where visitors have trouble orienting themselves may be popular ... on account of its quaint and exclusive character or because of other abstract qualities'. It is clearly important that we should not plan cities simply 'from the air', i.e. without a strong understanding of the functional as well as the visual qualities that lead to the formation of satisfying images. In existing cities, it is partly history that has led to a correlation between pleasing groundplans and interesting places. We have to learn a lot more about how to read the city image before we can translate our knowledge into city planning.

The identification of 'named parts'

Just as representation of the whole city shows the abstractions, distortions and regularities that characterize perceptual processes, named 'sub areas' induce their own unique images.

In a study of the urban Highgate Village, for example, although everyone 'knew' of its existence, there was no easy basis for drawing a sample of its residents. Some identified a small exclusive area and others (especially estate agents!) wanted to take advantage of its social cachet by stretching its boundaries as far as possible. Of the sample finally selected, about 80 per cent could draw the village on a map, but there was considerable variation in their boundaries. Apart from a central core area upon which most people agreed, residents tended to 'pull' the village towards their own homes.

The *city centre* of Karlsruhe as perceived by 1,000 of its citizens was studied by Klein (1967). The study demonstrates an alternative way of eliciting people's schemata or cognitive maps. Klein used 24 cards bearing the names of streets and landmarks and asked his subjects to 'pick out those which in your opinion are part of the town centre'. This method can be readily used to quantify the degree of consensus on boundaries and some of the functional origins of differences in perception of the city. People living nearer to the centre and those who had lived in the city for the longest period differentiated a smaller centre. Women had a larger area than men, for they tended to include an elegant shopping precinct and a cultural centre. There were also occupational differences, but the most interesting factor was that people living to the eastwards and westwards 'pulled' the city centre in their own direction and only quite a small area of overlap existed between them.

The urban neighbourhood

As with the city as a whole, the urban neighbourhood has been studied both by objective and subjective methods, i.e. 'on the ground' and 'in the mind'. The methods of the human ecologists, which consisted in the plotting of a variety of demographic statistics upon a map base, led to the designation of 'natural areas'. The best known studies were those in which statistics of crime, disease, divorce and other forms of morbidity were plotted so that areas where the rates were similar could be identified. This tradition has continued until the present day, passing through a stage called 'social area analysis' in which particular variables such as race and social class, which are judged to be socially important, are analysed in spatial terms by relating them to census enumeration districts. More recently, methods of *factorial ecology* have developed in which no prior dimensions are imposed upon the data but these are inductively extracted by factor analysis or by cluster analysis (see F1, E2).

Another form of the objective approach to neighbourhood study emerged in the *post war planning surveys* which were often conducted as a prelude to the replanning and rebuilding of cities in this country. The best example is probably the study of Middlesbrough carried out by Glass (1948). She used the method of superimposing a variety of indices and confirmed the existence in the city of about a dozen neighbourhoods which were defined as 'distinct by virtue of the special physical characteristics of the area and the specific social characteristics of its inhabitants'. However, recognizing the limitations of this definition of neighbourhood, Glass set up an alternative and more important definition of neighbourhood as follows: 'A territorial group, the members of which meet on common ground within their own area for primary

127

social activities and for organized and spontaneous social contacts.'

In order to test for the existence of this kind of grouping, the catchment areas were plotted of the schools, youth clubs, adult leisure activities, post offices and shops in the city. Regrettably, the overlap of these catchment areas was small and, more important, few of them showed much correspondence with the dozen or so neighbourhoods that had been identified using physical characteristics of the city and social characteristics of the residents. Indeed, it has been a recurrent difficulty with the objective approach that areas delineated by physical indices, such as rateable value, age and condition of housing, density of 'poverty shops' etc. do not correspond with social groupings. Since the latter are clearly more important, some sociologists have proposed the abandonment of 'sterile' attempts to define the boundaries of physical neighbourhoods.

This would seem wrong for several reasons. Most people actually construe neighbourhood in a territorial sense, e.g. 'the Jones' live in a nice neighbourhood'. Secondly, patterns of friendship in residential areas are invariably perceived as a part of a spatial framework. Even 'networks' (connected sets of friends), 'contact clusters' (places customarily visited) and 'communalities' (friendships based on shared interest as distinct from residential propinquity) imply a spatial patterning. Most important, however, friendship relationships may be the bones of neighbourhood, but they are certainly not the whole social body. This includes a great deal of mutual awareness and social conformity pressure based on communications that are non-verbal and often unconscious.

A possible resolution of this perplexing misfit between physical and social neighbourhood is offered by the subjective approach. This measures the neighbourhood through its representation in the mind of the resident. It is measured not at the behavioural but at the cognitive level.

Neighbourhood as a socio-spatial schema

Even as far back as the Chicago School, it was reckoned that urban residents must have a 'rudimentary sense of self-consciousness' of their natural area. Later, Sweetzer (1941) interviewed the 54 residents of a city block and made spatial plots of their friends and acquaintances within the block itself and facing streets. Instead of using the data to delineate a particular social neighbourhood, he adopted the important and novel concept of the *personal neighbourhood*. He concluded from his data that neighbourhoods are *compositionally* unique and *spatially* discontinuous. That is, each subject had a unique set of acquaintances, variously distributed; but he regarded the spaces between them as 'neutral'.

In a somewhat similar study about ten years later, a distinction was clearly drawn between neighbourhood consciousness and neighbourhood behaviour and when, in pursuit of the former, a sample were asked 'what do you consider your neighbourhood to be?' a large proportion answered in terms of contiguous housing blocks. These neighbourhoods were compositionally unique but *not* spatially discontinuous. The conflict over the latter characteristic may be said to have resulted directly from the way in which the questions were posed. Sweetzer had inferred the existence of a neighbourhood schema from a pattern of individual friendships; the later study elicited the schema directly from the residents.

The latter strategy was used in a study of neighbourhoods carried out by the author (Lee, 1954, 1968) in Cambridge. Residents were asked to 'please draw a line around the part which you consider acts as your neighbourhood or district' on an individual map which showed their house in the centre marked with a large cross and other details with sufficient clarity for all street names to be easily discernible. This was a technique evolved in the course of a piloting phase which began with open ended interviewing. During this intensive questioning it became apparent that the neighbourhood was extremely *salient* to people. Also that it comprised a synthesis of the multiplicity of both *social* and *physical* interactions between the person and the environment.

The subjects described graphically how their neighbourhood was formed by adding territory in order to include the neighbours who lived within it and by adding new neighbours because they occupied territory which itself was included by virtue of the physical facilities it afforded, such as playgrounds, telephone boxes, shops and, of course, houses of a particular style or socio-economic grade. Furthermore, their neighbour-hoods had all the characteristics of a *gestalt* (see A4). They were 'whole figures', standing out from the undifferentiated background; with 'form quality'; with contours that belong to the figure and not to the ground; they were more lively and articulated than the ground. The neighbourhoods were judged to be spatially continuous because although the residents' knowledge of and commitment to the social and physical area was uneven there was some kind of distinct relationship to the whole.

The concept used to describe neighbourhoods of this kind was the *socio-spatial schema*.

It should be stressed that it would be technically feasible to measure neighbourhoods like this at the response level of behaviour but it would be exceedingly laborious. It is more expedient to attempt to elicit their inner representation, the precipitate of cognitions and behavioural plans and expect-ancies that form as a result of a myriad interactions with people and place.

The neighbourhood maps of a representative sample of residents in the city were elicited at the same time as an inten-sive interview covering many aspects of behaviour in the urban environment. The superimposition of the maps showed that although there is some degree of agreement about major boundaries such as main roads, railways and rivers, the general effect is one of considerable variation. Indeed, the aggregated maps from the whole sample remind one of a plate of spaghetti!

The purpose of the analysis that followed was to try to discover whether any kind of order underlies the apparent diversity. But first the validity of the maps was cross-checked against the behavioural data by correlating their geographical size and various measures of physical composition against the subject's reported number of friendships in the locality, her use of local shops and membership in clubs and societies.

Since the maps were drawn in different parts of the city with widely divergent population density and physical com-position, standard measures of the latter characteristics were derived by drawing a circle of half mile radius about the subject's home at centre and analysing in detail the composi-tion of this territory. These measures represented the *imposed* environment or context to which the socio-spatial schema could be said to represent a response. It would be expected that the latter would also be partially influenced by characteristics of the subject herself, but a discussion of these relationships will be deferred until we have sketched in the social policy context within which the investigation was carried out.

The neighbourhood unit

The neighbourhood unit is a model for urban planning that is generally attributed to a book written in 1929 by Clarence A. Perry entitled *Man in the Machine Age*. In reaction against the drab deserts of mass housing that were spreading in cities, he proposed that neighbourhoods should be planned and built as a whole to endow a sense of identity and to promote feelings of community. They would have a central focus comprising a shopping precinct, school and community centre within easy walking distance for all residents. Access roads would converge towards the centre and major traffic routes would flank the unit so that children could reach school in comparative safety. Industry would be grouped at the edges of units and this, together with a generous provision of urban space, would help to accentuate their separation. The population would be a balanced mix of social classes and different interests.

The idea owed much to the success of the garden cities such as Letchworth and Welwyn, and it was influenced also by the University Settlement and Community Centre movements. However, it remained little more than a visionary panacea until the immediate post war years when it was adopted by the government as official policy, both for the New Towns and for all large scale residential development. While it could hardly be expected that these proposals would be incorporated in full, it was hoped that as many of its desirable features would be adopted as circumstances would allow. The advocated size of units was set at a population of 10,000 to 15,000.

Inevitably, there was opposition. The critics argued that the neighbourhood unit was quite unsuited to modern urban living which, they claimed, is anonymous, highly mobile and 'special interest' seeking! People no longer want to choose

131

their friends on the basis of proximity. The neighbourhood unit, they said, is 'village green' planning and 'bucolic nostalgia'.

The challenge for research was to explore whether urban neighbourhoods still exist and if so, what they are like.

Results of the Cambridge study.

The first of these questions has already been answered by the finding that a very high percentage of city residents apparently have a salient socio-spatial schema. The neighbourhood is real. For ordinary people (and especially for housewives and mothers who formed the subjects of this study) mobility is limited and much that they need can be located in a quite small local area.

Size, in fact, was one of the most consistent findings to emerge from the apparent chaos of neighbourhood maps. In spite of wide individual variation, the average area of the maps remains stable at about 100 acres in widely different parts of the city. Population density appears to have no effect on neighbourhood size. It follows that we should conceive of neighbourhoods in terms of geographical span and not, as proposed by the planners, in terms of the number of people they contain. Given the recommended gross population densities prevailing at the time (30 to 35 persons per acre) it required nearly 300 to 400 acres to enclose the prescribed number of people and it is hardly surprising that the residents rarely perceived them as meaningful units. Fortunately, density standards have now changed and it becomes possible to establish smaller units while still containing sufficient population to make viable provision for local shops and services. More recent designs have followed this trend.

By expressing the content (number of houses, shops and social buildings) of neighbourhood maps not in absolute terms but as a *proportion* of the content of the standard half mile radius, it was possible to correlate the composition of neighbourhoods as well as their size, with a number of characteristics. For example, differences with social class, age and length of residence were demonstrated and it was shown that having the wage earner working locally increased the likelihood of a housewife having a large physically varied neighbourhood and high social involvement. Living in a terraced house has a similar but much less pronounced influence, but being a native has the opposite effect. The latter result is mainly because natives and working class families have relatively small neighbourhoods and rely for their social integration on networks of kin spread throughout the city. Ownership of a car has no effect on neighbourhood, probably because the car's main significance is in establishing an additional schema (going for rides at the weekend within a range that makes it possible to get back in time to put the children to bed) rather than enlarging the urban neighbourhood. Finally, where social classes are mixed, it was shown that the neighbourhood involvement is somewhat greater.

The Murray

The Murray is a typical neighbourhood unit built in the Scottish New Town of East Kilbride. A study by Henry and Cox (1970) provides some useful confirmation of at least the negative aspects of the Cambridge study, i.e., the prediction that a neighbourhood of 300 acres (10,000 population) is much too large to provide a sense of identity – this despite the mention of its name under every street sign in the neighbourhood!

The residents were asked to trace the boundaries of The Murray over a street map of the whole town. No less than 90 per cent were able to attempt this, but there was wide variation in their schemata. They recognized the existence of a 'planner's neighbourhood' (which in our terminology might be regarded as a 'named part'), but according to the authors they also had a personal neighbourhood although this was not the subject of the investigation. The relative ineffectiveness of The Murray can be judged from the fact that despite its size, 63 per cent had a local pub outside its limits and more housewives used the town centre than the local shops.

Clintonville

An important study by Golledge and Zannaras (1973) of Clintonville, a suburb of Columbus, Ohio, deliberately explored the claim that the 'perceived neighbourhood' is a synthesis of physical and social space by asking their subjects to draw separate maps of each. They concluded that both '... do exist in the minds of respondents and can be identified as such, but that ... the degree of overlap is sufficient to warrant the statements made by other researchers, that the two are very closely linked in the mind of the urban dweller'. It is a difficulty of this approach that, if asked by a high status researcher to delineate two separate areas, most people would try to oblige and might think it discourteous to insist that the request was unrealistic.

This study also included an analysis by multiple regression, in which a large number of variables that could 'explain' the differences in the neighbourhood maps were ranked in order of their correlations or 'explanatory power'. The results show an impressive degree of concordance with the Cambridge study. Length of residence, social class, organizational affiliations, numbers of local friends and patronization of local shopping centres are all positively correlated with neighbourhood map size.

Home ranges, activity spaces and home areas

Several other concepts have been used in attempts to understand how people delineate their urban space. For example, the concept of *home range*, the area within which the majority of excursions is limited and hence also an area of familiarity, has been found useful in studying developmental changes in childhood and in comparing people from different ethnic groups. It is similar to the *social activity space* used by Buttimer (1972) in a study of Glasgow housing estates. She determined from interviews the range of three zones of local (e.g. shops), intermediate (e.g. doctor) and diffuse (e.g. distant social visiting) zones of activity and aggregated the results for each of the zones, using a statistical method that summarizes their average span and directional coordinates. This made it possible to compare old with new and peripheral with central housing estates in the city.

Yet another concept has been the *home area* which is a subjective territory elicited in a similar way to the personal neighbourhood and probably closely corresponding to it. Its significance lies in the fact that it was applied to a national sample of over 2,000 people as part of the support research for the Royal Commission on Local Government (1969). The respondents were asked; 'is there an area round here, where you are now living, which you would say you belonged to and where you feel at home'. The findings confirmed the reality of diverse schemata, and showed most of them to be smaller than the currently existing local government areas. Since the legislation that eventually followed has drastically enlarged these areas it must be presumed that the implications were ignored, or considered less important than other factors.

It is important to realize that the whole of a city is segmented into 'named parts', such as Mayfair, Knightsbridge, Limehouse, Aldgate, often with superordinate parts such as West End and East End, and subordinate ones that consist of smaller areas or street names. The need for this is clearly that a complex environment has to be subdivided into districts and labelled in a shared frame of reference so that people can communicate with each other. Questions such as 'where is it'? and 'where do you live'? can only be answered by reference to such a system. It is interesting that the labelling is adjusted in use to synchronize communication. If a New Yorker asks an Englishman where he lives, he may get the reply 'London'; but if a person from Shoreditch puts the same question, he is more likely to get the reply 'Streatham'. The boundaries of both districts are equivocal because of individual differences in the images, but their use is essential to social orientation. They should be distinguished from personal neighbourhoods, which may be influenced by a 'named part' but do not necessarily correspond to it. As was seen with the residents of The Murray, people are perfectly capable of maintaining two systems, the one for personal or family use and the other for public use.

Conclusion

This brief conclusion must serve as an epilogue not only for Chapter 7 but for the remainder of this small volume. No attempt has been made to round off individual chapters because each of the areas covered is at so early and still fragmentary a stage of development that a circumspective view of each would be premature. The scattered empirical evidence must speak for itself.

Nonetheless, it is hoped that the wider, exciting, enterprise of environmental psychology has assumed some shape and character in the preceding pages. It is hoped that the objectives, at least, have become plain and been found worthwhile. The task of applying the methods of science towards an understanding of man–environment interaction is a considerable challenge. If we can master it, and match our knowledge to our burgeoning technology, we shall perhaps be able to navigate ourselves in space a little nearer to the realization of our values.

Subject Index

References and
Name Index

The numbers in italics following each entry refer to page numbers within this book.

Allport, F. H. (1920) The influence of the group upon association and thought. *Journal of Experimental Psychology 3*: 159–82. *80*

Altman, I. (1975) *The Environment and Social Behavior*. Belmont, California: Wadsworth. *21, 40*

Appleyard, D. Styles and methods of structuring a city. *Environment and Behaviour 2*: 100–17. *125*

Barker, R. G. and Gump, P. V. (eds) (1964) *Big School, Small School: High School Size and Student Behavior*. Stanford: University Press. *99*

Barker, R. G. (1968) *Ecological Psychology*. Stanford: University Press. *31, 99*

Bartlett, F. C. (1932) *Remembering*. Cambridge: University Press. *35, 122*

Baxter, J. C. (1970) Interpersonal spacing in natural settings. *Sociometry 33*: 444–56. *58*

Bergum, B. O. and Lehr, D. J. (1963) Effects of authoritarianism on vigilance performance. *Journal of Applied Psychology 47*: 75–7. *81*

Breux, J. J. (1974) Factors affecting social contagion in crowds. D. Phil. Dissertation, University of Oxford. *58*

Buttimer, A. (1972) Social space and the planning of residential areas. *Environment and Behavior 4*: 279–318. *134*

Canter, D. V. (1969) The psychological implications of office size. Ph.D. Dissertation, University of Liverpool. *93*

Canter, D. V. (1970) Need for a theory of function in architecture. *Architects' Journal*, 4.2.70: 299–302. *13*

Canter, D. V. (1972) Royal Hospital for Sick Children. *Architects' Journal*, 6.9.72: 525–64. *113*

Canter, D. V. (1974) *Psychology for Architects*. London: Applied Science Publishers. *48*

Cook, J. (1969) Do the gardens fit the people. *New Society*, 17.4.69. *76*

Henry, L. and Cox, P. A. (1970) The neighbourhood concept in new town planning: a perception study in East Kilbride. *Horizon 19*: 37–45. *133*

Craik, K. H. (1973) Environmental psychology. *Annual Review of Psychology 24*: 403–22. *17*

De Jonge, D. (1962) Images of urban areas: their structure and psychological foundations. *Journal of American Institute of Planners 28*: 266–76. *125*

Durlak, J. T. and Lehman, J. (1974) User awareness and sensitivity to open space: a study of traditional and open plan schools. In D. V. Canter and T. R. Lee (eds) *Psychology and the Built Environment*. London: Architectural Press (pp. 164–9). *88*

Edwards, M. (1974) Comparison of some expectations of a sample of housing architects with known data. In D. V. Canter and T. R. Lee (eds) *Psychology and the Built Environment*. London: Architectural Press (pp. 38–47). *68*

Foot, H. C. and Lee, T. R. (1970) Social feedback in the learning of a motor skill. *British Journal of Social and Clinical Psychology 9*: 309–19. *83*

Garbarino, J. (1975) *Megalopolis and the high school as a socialising agency*. Paper read at I.S.S.B.D. Conference, University of Surrey, July 1975. *99*

Glass, R. (1948) *The Social Background of a Plan: A Study of Middlesbrough*. London: Routledge & Kegan Paul. *127*

Gibson, E. J. (1969) *Principles of Perceptual Learning and Development*. New York: Appleton–Century–Crofts. *122*

Goffman, E. (1959) *The Presentation of Self in Everyaay Life*. New York: Doubleday/Anchor. *106*

Goffman, E. (1963) *Behaviour in Public Places*. New York: The Free Press. *70*

Golledge, R. G. and Zannaras, G. (1973) Cognitive approaches to the analysis of human spatial behavior. In W. H. Ittelson (ed.) *Environment and Cognition*. New York: Seminar Press. *133*

Griffiths, I. D. and McIntyre, D. A. (1971) *A Factor Analysis of Subjective Ratings of the Thermal Environment*. Chester: Electricity Council Research Centre, Note 399. *95*

Grindley, G. C. (1932) The formation of a simple habit in guinea pigs. *British Journal of Psychology 23*: 127–47. *29*

Gurnee, H. (1962) *Group Learning*. Psychological Monographs 76, No. 13. *84*

Hediger, H. (1950) *Wild Animals in Captivity*. London: Butterworth. *41*

Holahan, C. J. and Saegert, S. (1973) Behavioral and attidudinal effects of large scale variation in the physical environment of psychiatric wards. *Journal of Abnormal Psychology 82*: 454–62. *113*

Horowitz, M. J., Duff, D. and Stratton, L. (1964) Body buffer zone. *Archives of General Psychiatry 11*: 651–6. *111*

Hall, E. T. (1966) *The Hidden Dimension.* London: Bodley Head. *39*

Hull, C. L. (1943) *Principles of Behavior.* New York: Appleton-Century. *120*

Humphreys, M. A. (1974) Relating wind rain and temperature to teachers' reports of young children's behaviour. In D. V. Canter and T. R. Lee (eds) *Psychology and the Built Environment.* London: Architectural Press (pp. 19–28). *96*

Ittelson, W. H., Proshansky, H. M. and Rivlin, L. G. (1970) The environmental psychology of the psychiatric ward. In H. M. Proshansky *et al.* (eds) *Environmental Psychology.* New York: Holt, Rinehart & Winston (pp. 419–39). *112*

Jourard, S. M. (1966) An exploratory study of body-accessibility. *British Journal of Social and Clinical Psychology 5*: 221–31. *40*

Kira, A. (1957). The bathroom. *Center for Housing and Environmental Studies, Cornell University, Research report No. 7. 67*

Kelly, G. A. (1955) *The Psychology of Personal Constructs.* Vols. 1 & 2. New York: Norton. *32, 114*

Keuthe, J. L. (1962) Social schemas. *Journal of Abnormal and Social Psychology 64*: 31–8. *59*

Klein, A. J. (1967) The delimitation of the town centre in the images of its citizens. *Urban Core and Inner City.* Leiden: Brill (pp. 286–306). *126*

Laumann, E. O. and House, J. S. (1970) Living room styles and social attributes: the patterning of material artifacts in a modern urban community. *Sociology and Social Research 54*: 321–42. *63*

Leavitt, H. (1951) Some effects of certain communication patterns on group performance. *Journal of Abnormal and Social Psychology 46*: 38–50. *84*

Lee, T. R. (1954) *A Study of Urban Neighbourhood.* Ph.D. Dissertation, University of Cambridge. *34, 129*

Lee, T. R. (1957) On the relation between the school journey and social and emotional adjustment in rural infant children. *British Journal of Educational Psychology 27*: 101–14. *102*

Lee, T. R. (1961) A test of the hypothesis that school reorganization is a cause of rural depopulation. *Durham Research Review 3*: 64–73. *101*

Lee, T. R. (1963) The optimum provision and siting of social clubs. *Durham Research Review 14*: 53–61. *53*

Lee, T. R. (1968) Urban neighbourhood as a socio-spatial schema. *Human Relations 21*: 241–267. *129*

Lee, T. R. (1971) Psychology and architectural determinism. *Architects Journal* 4.8.71; 1.9.71; 22.9.71. *22*

Lee, T. R., Tagg, S. K., and Abbott, D. J. (1975) *Social Severance by Urban Roads and Motorways.* Proceedings of Patrac Symposium on Environmental Evaluation. London: HMSO (to appear). *50*

Lewin, K. (1936) *Principles of Topological Psychology*. New York: McGraw Hill. *28*

Lynch, K. (1960) *The Image of the City*. Cambridge, Mass.: M.I.T. Press. *124*

Madge, C. (1951) Private and public spaces. *Human Relations 3*: 187–99. *26*

Mehrabian, A. and Russell, J. (1974) *An Approach to Environmental Psychology*. Cambridge, Mass.: M.I.T. Press. *57*

Milgram, S. (1965) Some conditions of obedience and disobedience to authority. *Human Relations 18*: 57–76. *81*

Mintz, N. L. (1956) Effects of aesthetic surroundings. *Journal of Psychology 41*: 459–66. *72*

Paivio, A. (1971) *Imagery and Verbal Processes*. New York: Holt, Rinehart & Winston. *123*

Perin, C. (1970) *With Man in Mind*. Cambridge, Mass.: M.I.T. Press. *13*

Perlmutter, H. V. and De Montmollin, G. (1952) Group learning of nonsense syllables. *Journal of Abnormal and Social Psychology 47*: 762–9. *84*

Perrin, F. A. C. (1914) *An Experimental and Introspective Study of the Human Learning Process in the Maze*. Psychological Monographs, 16: 70. *120*

Rapoport, A. (1969) *House Form and Culture*. Englewood Cliffs, N.J.: Prentice Hall. *66*

Rosengren, W. R. and De Vault, S. (1963) The sociology of time and space in an obstetrical hospital. In H. M. Proshansky *et al.* (eds) *Environmental Psychology*. New York: Holt, Rinehart & Winston (pp. 439–52). *105*

Royal Commission on Local Government (1969) *Research Studies, 9: Community Attitudes Survey*. London: HMSO. *134*

Saville, A. J. (1970) Technical studies of kitchen work top heights. *Architects' Journal 152*, no. 39 (30.9.70). *66*

Shepard, R. N. and Metzler, J. (1971) Mental rotation of three-dimensional objects. *Science 171*: 701–3. *123*

Smith, P. K. (1974) Aspects of the playgroup environment. In D. V. Canter and T. R. Lee (eds) *Psychology and the Built Environment*. London: Architectural Press (pp. 56–62). *86*

Smith, R. H., Lynch, M. T. and Downer, D. B. (1969) Physical space and living pattern relationships. *Journal of Home Economics 61*: 429–32. *79*

Sommer, R. (1967) Sociofugal space. *American Journal of Sociology 72*: 654–60. *92*

Sommer, R. (1970) The ecology of study areas. *Environment and Behaviour 2*: 271–80. *94*

Sommer, R. and Peterson, P. (1967) Study of careers re-examined. *College and Research Libraries* July, 263–72. *94*

Spivack, M. (1967) Sensory distortions in tunnels and corridors. *Hospital and Community Psychiatry 18*: 24–30. *110*

Start, K. B. and Richardson, A. (1964) Imagery and mental practice. *British Journal of Educational Psychology 34*: 280–4. *123*

Stebbins, R. A. (1973) Physical context influences on behaviour: the case of classroom disorderliness. *Environment and Behavior 5*: 291. *97*

Stringer, P. (1970) Architecture, psychology, the game's the same. In D. V. Canter (ed) *Architectural Psychology*. London: RIBA Publications (pp. 7–11). *33*

Stringer, P. (1974) Individual differences in repertory grid measures for a cross section of the female population. In D. V. Canter and T. R. Lee (eds) *Psychology and the Built Environment*. London: Architectural Press (pp. 96–104). *34*

Studer, R. G. (1969) The dynamics of behaviour-contingent physical systems. In H. M. Proshansky, W. H. Ittelson and L. G. Rivlin (eds) *Environmental Psychology, Man and his Physical Settings*. New York: Holt, Rinehart & Winston (pp. 56–75). *30*

Sweetzer, F. L. (1941) *Neighbourhood Acquaintance and Association: A Study of Personal Neighbourhoods*. Ph.D. Thesis, Faculty of Political Science, Columbia University, N.Y. *129*

Tolman, E. C. (1932) *Purposive Behaviour in Animals and Men*. New York: Appleton–Century–Crofts. *120*

Triplett, N. (1897) The dynamogenic factors in pacemaking and competition. *American Journal of Psychology 9*: 507–33. *80*

Trites, D. K., Galbraith, F. D., Sturdevant, M. and Leckwary, J. F. (1970) Influence of nursing-unit design on the activities and subjective feelings of nursing personnel. *Environment and Behaviour 11*: 303–34. *109*

Wapner, S. and Alper, T. (1952) The effect of an audience on behaviour in a choice situation. *Journal of Abnormal and Social Psychology 47*: 222–9. *81*

Wools, R. (1970) The assessment of room friendliness. In D. V. Canter (ed.) *Architectural Psychology*. London: RIBA Publications (pp. 48–55). *48*

Wools, R. and Canter, D. V. (1970) The effects of the meaning of buildings on behaviour. *Applied Ergonomics 1*: 144–50. *72*